No Looking

Marilyn Stowe's essential guide for
surviving divorce and building a life beyond

Acknowledgements:

There are so many people I wish to thank for their love, help and support and these include (in no particular order) Suzanne, Jeffrey, Debra, Rebecca, Abigail, Leah, Joshua, Freddie, Louise and Susan (who each deserve at least a VC for services above and beyond the call of duty and for valour) and not forgetting Monty, all my fantastic friends and colleagues at Grahame Stowe Bateson, particularly the Family Law Unit at Temple Bar, my equally fantastic colleagues and friends from the Law Society's Family Law Panel, Irene who was instrumental in persuading me to 'have a go with a 2nd book', to Peter my friend and trusted adviser through the years and above all my thanks to my clients, who have voted with their feet, put their trust in me and my practise and to whom I remain truly indebted and deeply grateful. Finally, my most heartfelt and special thanks to the two special men in my life, my 'senior' partner, a tower of strength who puts up with far more than he should, (but look at the benefits?) and Ben, whose sunny disposition (and he needs it) has made our life complete.

Marilyn Stowe
July 2002

Disclaimer

The contents of this book are intended as general advice and guidance only. Readers should not place any personal reliance on the material, particularly as the law in this area is constantly changing. For specific advice, consult a solicitor.

The case studies mentioned in this book are intended as examples only and do not refer to any actual people, alive or dead.

First published July 2002

ISBN 0-9543082-0-4

For my parents, Arnold and Estelle Morris with much love and gratitude.

Contents

Introduction

The state we're in

Divorce is like sex. Everyone seems to be doing it. At least that's the way it can appear. The Royals do it. Hollywood stars make a habit of it. Politicians do it, sports stars, television personalities, writers, academics and business leaders all do it. It's likely to have happened to members of your family and to many of your friends. In the year 2000, the last year for which official figures are available, there were 141,135 divorces granted in England and Wales compared to 267,961 marriages. So, if it's happening to you, you're not odd, you're not unusual and you're certainly not alone. And, painful though the experience may initially be, your life is not over. There is a life beyond the pain and the tears and, compared to previous generations of women, you will get a better deal if your marriage ends.

I have been a divorce lawyer for more than 20 years. In that time I have handled thousands of cases. Nothing shocks me any more. Nothing surprises me about the way one human being can treat another. I have learned that there is no absolute fault and no total innocence when a relationship falls apart. I know I have become harder during that time. I have to keep a professional detachment to be able to perform my job most effectively. I am afraid to say that I now have little patience with people who insist only on looking back, who continue to live in a past that has gone forever. It is not a question of being unsympathetic but rather one of encouraging my client to deal with the reality of their new situation.

Believe it or not, I am a romantic at heart. I believe in love and I believe that marriage should be for life. But when it goes wrong I also believe there is no point in prolonging the hurt. No-one, least of all Government, has the right to tell people how to live their lives or to force them to stay together when they want to be apart. I don't believe anyone gets married thinking they will one day get divorced. But it has become an increasingly common aspect of our society. Love fades, people change, circumstances alter and individuals grow and develop in unexpected and unintended ways. Ending a relationship calls first for the acceptance of some harsh facts. The marriage is OVER. Your partner no longer WANTS you. The life you had is GONE. I don't believe in trying to prolong relationships that are dead. My role is to extricate my client from the marriage as quickly and painlessly as possible and with the most advantageous financial arrangements in place. I have earned the nickname, 'The Barracuda' among certain fellow lawyers because they know that, if necessary and amicable negotiations have failed, I will fight tooth and nail for my client. Then I will encourage them to grab hold of their new life with both hands.

It's not easy and it is not painless. But the alternative is simply too depressing to contemplate. It is often a state of mind. A woman who has been married for most of her adult life may well find it daunting to imagine starting again alone, no matter how unsatisfactory the marriage was. The fact that she was Mrs Somebody gave her a role and stature in life. Without that title she feels anonymous, unsure about her place in society and, let's be honest, frightened. The older she is and the longer the marriage has lasted, the more intense those feelings are sure to be. But the lot of the divorced woman today is infinitely better than that faced by previous generations. Changing social attitudes, women's increasing financial independence and a fairer approach in law have all contributed to a more enlightened environment.

The whole process of divorce is far improved on what once pertained. The process has been streamlined so that a routine, agreed divorce can be concluded, from the initial step of lodging the petition through granting of the decree nisi to it being made absolute, within three or four months. Changes in legislation have also resulted in wives getting a more equitable financial deal when their marriages break down. Children are no longer treated as assets to be 'owned' by one party or the other. It has also been recognised, and not before time, that fathers have rights too and that it is not always best that children live with their mother. There has been a concerted effort on the part of the Government and all the professionals involved to remove the bitterness and aggression out of the process, as far as is humanly possible. Amicable settlements are now the aim. And to a large degree that is working. It is now very rare to get a defended divorce going to court. The concept of 'fault' is largely irrelevant. It is now commonly recognised that there are no pure saints and no total sinners in relationships. Blame and fault normally come in now only when one party wishes to prove an irretrievable breakdown to secure an immediate divorce and cites unreasonable behaviour or adultery.

Almost half of all marriages in this country now end in divorce. Although actual numbers of divorces declined each year since 1997, when they stood at 146,689 to 2000 when there were 141,135, the number of marriages has also been falling in line.

And the cost of divorce to the national economy, however, is staggering. The annual legal aid bill for matrimonial and family proceedings is running at around £387 million a year with the full cost to the public purse of the fall-out from divorce estimated at around £5 billion a year. The emotional cost is harder to quantify. For instance, there were 142,457 children aged under 16 who were in families where the parents divorced in 2000. Given the fact that divorce rates were highest among men and women aged between 25 and 29, it is not surprising to learn that a quarter , almost 36,000, of those were children aged under 5 years.

There are other costs too. It is estimated that 43% of all violent crime experienced by women is domestic. In 1997 for example, of 224 female murder victims, almost half were killed by their current or former partners.

There are many commentators who throw up their hands in horror at these figures and call for divorce to be made harder. They are missing the point entirely. When two people no longer wish to live together then they should be helped to end the marriage as quickly and painlessly and possible and to move on with their lives. No, it's not divorce that should be made harder, it's marriage that should be more difficult, the result of serious thought and consideration and not just a whim. The whole concept of family and relationships is changing. Just two stories in the weekend papers as I wrote the final chapters of this book confirmed that. One gave details of a scientific breakthrough in the development of 'artificial' sperm that would enable , for instance, two women to have a baby together without any male involvement at all and the other was about a plan by one of the leading supermarket chains to enable their customers to file for divorce at the same time as doing their grocery shopping.

However, despite all that I believe that marriage is here to stay. And the statistics seem to confirm that. The number of marriages rose by almost 2% in the year 2000. There are many possible explanations; some people even attribute the example of Posh 'n' Becks as a positive role model for the young. But if marriage is here to say, then so is divorce. More of us will be married more than once in our lives. We may end up divorced more than once too.

Should it happen to you, this book is meant to help you through divorce and out the other side intact as a human being, sadder maybe, wiser definitely and better able to build a new life.

PART I
The Way we Live and Love Today

1. Staying together or moving on

Unless they are a very devious and unscrupulous individual, no-one gets married planning for the divorce. When couples pledge 'until death us do part' they tend to mean it. But life brings unexpected temptations and unforeseen pressures. People change. Relationships wither. Although I believe that divorce should be easier it shouldn't be the first resort. Every avenue should be explored before the decision is made to bring the marriage to an end.

The real problem is recognising when the marriage is first beginning to go wrong and deciding, as a couple, to do something about it. If only one of you wants to save the relationship, then it just won't work. It can only be rescued and revived if both parties believe the relationship is worth fighting for. And then it can work only if both parties are committed. Very often the ultimate reason for the marriage failure is, in fact, only a symptom of the breakdown rather than the cause. For example, an adulterous affair which brings about a divorce may well have arisen because the marriage has, to all intents and purposes, already broken down although the actual affair itself is not the initial cause.

It's rare that marriages collapse suddenly. They tend to wither over a protracted period. Couples lose interest in each other. They take each other for granted. They stop trying. We've all seen such couples in the High Street. She's in full make up and looking smart; he's slobbing alongside, unshaven and wearing a scruffy tracksuit and trainers. There will be feelings of resentment, isolation, anger, frustration and there will also be a lack of interest both sexually and mentally. Boredom is likely to set in and ultimately the temptation may arise which proves too difficult to resist. Of course a marriage which on the surface appears to be completely happy may be disrupted by the intervention of a third party, even though such an event was never actively sought or anticipated by the husband or wife.

That is simply unlucky and whichever party is unwilling or unable to resist the charms and attractions of a third party will often say he or she never intended it to happen. They may even be genuinely sorry that it did. Nevertheless the damage has been done. It has destroyed the trust that glued the marriage together. Both parties now consider it over and want out. Such cases in my opinion are not in the majority. Most marriages break down over a longer period of time and for a multitude of reasons.

The question is how to recognise the problems and what to do about them. At the end of the day the grass elsewhere is not as green as it may seem. A second marriage is just as likely to founder as the first (if not more likely) and, even as a hardened divorce lawyer often accused of cynicism, I would advocate holding a marriage together at whatever cost, assuming the co-operation and willingness of both parties. There is a world of difference between a genuine desire to work to save a marriage when it is the shared aim of both parties, and a hope and a prayer existing only in the mind of one.

I do not like the concept of separation. For me separation is a halfway house which offers little if any consolation to either party. It is not necessary for divorce. That is a myth which is perpetuated by every pub lawyer that I come across. (Two years of separation, providing both parties consent, can be valid grounds for divorce. If there is no consent, then the couple must live apart for five years before one of them can seek a divorce against the other's will. There are other grounds which may also exist prior to a period of separation.) In my opinion during a separation it is impossible to recover from the effect of a broken relationship purely because the divorce has not taken place. Both parties are leading completely separate lives, meeting different people and perhaps becoming involved romantically again - yet at the same time they are not free, whether they consented to a separation or not. Perhaps one party may cling to the thought of an ultimate reconciliation. Very often the one has decided the marriage has come to an end can't bring him- or herself - to tell their partner the harsh truth. Instead he or she hides behind the charade of a separation. 'Let's see how it works out for the next few months,' he or she says, holding out false hopes and dreams to the partner, only to shatter them months later, at substantial emotional cost to the person who worries and waits in a timewarp, refusing to accept the blindingly obvious.

I believe that if a marriage is going to succeed it does so with both parties living together. If neither party can live with the other or if one party feels that the marriage is over then by far the kindest way out is to end that marriage as quickly as possible. Sometimes it is necessary to be cruel to be kind.

2. Early warning signs

After 20 years as a divorce lawyer, I've heard all the excuses and all the explanations. Given that we are all different as individuals, it is surprising how many of us tend to follow the same habitual patterns of behaviour. I thought it might be useful here, and only slightly tongue in cheek, to use all those years of experience to set down the most common ways that he can tell you're cheating on him. In the interests of sexual equality, I should also explain how he can tell you might be being unfaithful too.

Ten ways to tell he's cheating on you

1. He starts taking unusual interest in his clothes and overall appearance!
You've nagged him for years about those boring suits and stained ties. You've urged him to adopt a more trendy hairstyle and told him that excessive amount of unwanted facial and nasal hair really aren't a turn-on. Now he's taking action on his own that should start the alarm bells ringing.

2. He takes out new credit cards in his name only and you never see the monthly bills.
A sure sign he's spending money on things he doesn't want you to know about. He's probably going to try and claim some of the expenses on his business so he'll be keeping the receipts somewhere!

3. He suddenly starts spending nights away from home 'on business'
He says his new position at work means having to travel more frequently. And don't call him at the hotel as he will be with clients all night. He'll call you when he's free. Oh yeah?

4. He takes an unusual amount of interest in how effective your diet is and signs up at the local gym!
After years when his only exercise was carrying his beer to the seat in front of the television to watch football, he is now desperate to regain his youth. And you know why!

5. He starts to make snide and hurtful remarks about you and your views when in company!

Feeling guilty about his affair, the only way he can justify it to himself is by pretending you forced him into it by treating him badly. If his comments goad you into responding in kind he can convince himself its all your fault.

6. He starts to drop the name of a female colleague into everyday conversation in flattering ways!

Subconsciously he's comparing her with you so just dropping her name in conversation makes her superior. And it gives him a feeling of power. ' I'm so clever/powerful that I can even drop the name of my mistress in conversation at home and not get found out.' Men can be so stupid!

7. He starts intercepting the postman and says he'll check the bank statements during a spare half hour at work!

He's read all about those guys who get caught out by their wives finding hotel receipts in their suit pockets when taking clothes to the cleaners, so he's paying for everything in cash. If he keeps the bank statements you won't find out how many time's he's visiting the cashpoint.

8. He decides to trade in the family saloon for something a little more sporty!

The Ford/Vauxhall has always suited you in the past but now he says its time to start enjoying yourselves because the kids have grown up and you just don't need a family saloon. James at work says the Porsche Boxster is just so much fun and so economical to run. But just you try asking to borrow it for an evening!

9. He suggests separate holidays!

He's so busy at work that he can't take the time for a holiday. But you and kids should go; you can even take your parents and he'll pay. While you're away he won't have to rush off early from those illicit meetings with his lover.

10. Sex is a definite no no!

Even he won't try the headache routine; it's just not the kind of thing a `macho stud' like him would say. However, he is just so understanding and knows you're tired/ had a bad day/ got an early start. Anything to avoid physical contact.

Ten ways he can tell you're cheating on him

1. The mobile phone bill goes missing!

If you're talking endlessly to your lover, the last thing you want is for him to check the increasing phone bill and find out its nearly all down to calls to one number. Worse than that, you definitely don't want him calling that number!

2. You don't cook for him any more!

When he gets home and asks what you've made for dinner and you reply, 'I've made reservations' he knows he's in trouble.

3. You start to talk excessively about how good the window cleaner is,

how the tennis coach has really improved your game or why the builders need to stay longer than intended! The wives of rich and successful men who feel neglected and second best to the attractions of work, often find solace with a lover of far less material wealth, someone who substitutes financial rewards for real attention.

4. You really don't care how his day went at work!

The conversation and gossip from work you once found fascinating and witty now bores you to tears. You're no longer interested in his work because you're no longer interested in him and it shows.

5. You look trimmer, slimmer and younger and he still hasn't noticed!

If he no longer notices your hair, make-up or figure he probably won't realise you've found someone else who does. By the time he gets round to realising that someone else finds you attractive it'll be too late. The excitement of the new will make him look very old hat and boring indeed.

6. You're suddenly spending more time with girlfriends .
You suggest you should have a separate bank account for those little 'girly' indulgences without having to bother him all the time. At least that's what you want him to believe. But does he really think you'd get that dressed up and that excited over a pizza and a glass of wine with all-female company? And what about when he tries to find your bank statements or discover your pin number?

7. You are unusually understanding when work means he can't make the holiday you've arranged. Will he really believe you when you say you'll go anyway and enjoy the sun and read all those books you never got round to! You may tell him you're in Bournemouth but actually you've gone back to Barbados to meet the guy he had dismissed as a beach bum on your last trip together to the Caribbean. But don't get caught out by letting him phone you. Tell him you know he's too busy to call and you'll ring him. That way, he won't know where you're calling from.

8. You start to wear younger, sexier clothing and underwear and all he can do is moan about the cost!
He's long past noticing anything new you wear but there's a certain some-body who appreciates the efforts you make, isn't there? Just watch out if you use the joint account to pay for them. Make sure you tell him what you've bought even if you don't tell him why.

9. You feel embarrassed in his company!
All of a sudden he can't do anything right in your eyes; his fashion sense belongs in a different age, his jokes aren't funny any more and you start to compare him – unfavourably – with younger, slimmer more dynamic and successful friends and colleagues. If you want to keep that affair secret, you're going to have to hide these feelings.

10. Sex is a definite no no!
Okay, the headache excuse is so see-through its transparent and you've tried the one about being worried the children might hear, you're just too

tired because of the gym/tennis or there's a late night tv programme you just can't miss. Eventually the excuses will run out so you're going to have to decide to stay or go.

3. Making marriage harder and divorce easier

The debate about the make-up of the modern family generates heated comments whenever it flares up. Views are equally strongly held by those on both sides of the divide. The traditionalists believe that the perfect environment for nurturing children is a loving and legal family unit consisting of a married mother and father and their 2.1 children. The 'nuclear family' as it used to be called. On the other side of the debate are those who like to think of themselves as modern, liberal-minded free-thinkers. They don't believe it necessary to have a legal document to create a happy family. For them, it's love not the law that counts. Some go even further and believe that it is every woman's right to bear children, whether they chose to have a male partner or not. The future of the family is one of the most fiercely argued debates in society today. So what can we do about it? Could legislation help or is an ever-increasing rate of divorce simply a necessary evil that has come about as a result of our moves towards a more liberal society? The general consensus of opinion seems to be that divorce has been made too easy, that couples no longer see marriage as a lifetime commitment because it is relatively painless to escape from when things get a bit rough.

At the risk of running in the face of current opinion, I would say that this argument is absolute nonsense. No-one enjoys a divorce. I have yet to meet anyone who has been through the process and would describe it as easy. Despite changes and modifications, it is still far too difficult and I would advocate a further easing of the divorce laws without a moment's hesitation. This might raise the divorce rates even higher if this was the only change in legislation. But alongside this, I would propose making it a great deal harder to get married than it ever has been in the past

Getting married is simply too easy. If you have your parent's consent you are allowed to marry before you can legally drink, drive, vote or even watch a Mel Gibson movie. This is not to say that all divorces are as a result of young marriages. However old and wise you may be, the three weeks that it takes from registering your wish to wed to walking out of the Register Office as husband and wife is surely not enough.

If it takes twenty-one days to marry and two years to get an amicable divorce there must be imbalance in there somewhere! It's like giving people driving licences after a couple of lessons and then protesting that there are far too many accidents - it's a recipe for disaster. We should be looking at the cause, not the symptom. If we are to allow divorce at all then there are bound to be divorces. Statistics show that children of divorced parents are more likely to have failed marriages themselves, so the divorce rates will rise. To compensate for this, we must ensure that marriage is not entered into as lightly as it is at present.

The two years which couples have to wait before they can get a divorce via separation with consent, might not be such a bad ruling to apply to marriage. Or perhaps those intending to tie the knot should be made to visit pre-marital guidance counsellors, who would assume a similar role to that of vicar or priest in asking the couple whether they fully understand the implication of the vows they are taking. An even more radical idea, certainly cheaper than divorce, would be to charge £500 for the marriage licence! While this is not an entirely serious suggestion – although most young couples wouldn't think twice about paying such a sum for a new television or a two week holiday in the sun - major steps must be taken soon to help people avoid those marriages that are destined to fail. Increasingly, issues such as marriage, money, children, relationships and fidelity are on the curriculum in our schools. I believe they should form an obligatory 'Life-Skills' GCSE course for schoolchildren, along with home economics and advice about birth control. Why not? What is there to lose? Surely it is better to make our youth understand that marriage is much more than a fairy tale wedding. The more they know the less mistakes they are likely to make!

Like all cautionary tales, there is a great deal of truth in the old saying 'marry in haste, repent at leisure'. Marriage used to be, and still ought to be entered into with considerable thought and the belief that it is for life.

Of course whatever rules are laid down and whatever advice is offered, people are always going to make mistakes. But nine times out of ten, the mistake is going to be the marriage itself, not the divorce.

4. Having it all – the modern myth?

Britain has one of the highest divorce rates in Europe. The statistics are horrifying but they no longer shock. And yet the consequences are truly alarming. The cost in terms of public spending as a result of the increase in divorce is apparently running at over three billion pounds per annum. We are implored by the Government and other bodies to remember that the sanctity of the family is paramount, that everything possible should be done to keep a marriage ongoing with the family living together as one unit rather than two.

What has caused such an alarming state of affairs? I believe one of the major reasons arises out of a fundamental change which has occurred in our society particularly over the last twenty years.

The suffragettes fought hard for women's emancipation. They were prepared to chain themselves to railings and to be imprisoned in order to pursue women's rights. They simply would not recognise the lot of their sisters today. Women now stand alongside men as equals in many aspects of life. Women are now members of the professions, they hold jobs alongside men in the police force and fire services. They even get sent out to fight in war. One woman has been our prime minister. Women such as Madonna, Hilary Clinton and Cherie Blair are held up as role models. Women have striven to be treated like men and to a great extent this is exactly what they have achieved.

But at what price? The change in the woman's role means that it is now the norm and that most women will go out to work regardless of whether or not they also have a family and a home to look after. Indeed, it's almost expected. The full-time mother is something of an oddity today.

Why do women want to be like men? I believe that such a desire is in fact one of the major reasons for such overwhelming statistics on the breakdown of marriage. With the number of women going out to work comes the huge increase in numbers of broken families.

But why? For years I have been acting for working women who seek divorce because they can no longer take the pressure. Consider the day of an average working woman. She will usually prepare the breakfast and get the children ready for school. If she has time she will get herself ready for work as nicely as she can. She will probably take the children to school and rush off to work. In her lunch hour she will go shopping in the supermarket. At the end of work she will rush off again to the children, make them their tea, tidy up the house, do some washing and ironing and make dinner for herself and her husband. She might supervise the children's homework, bathe them and put them to bed. She will try to be pleasant to her husband. She will probably fall into bed exhausted - 'no sex tonight, thank you.' This pattern is repeated five days a week and at the weekend there is the family shop, catching up on the outstanding washing and ironing and giving the house a good clean. Then there is the gardening and all the other incidental chores that every housewife and mother knows only too well. If there are financial problems they will compound the pressure and stress. If a child falls ill then for a working mother this is tantamount to disaster. How is she supposed to cope? Come the school holidays the pressure continues at an even greater pace-who will look after the children, how will they manage? How can she tear herself in two between work and looking after the children? And if she does stop working how will the family manage financially? The strain of the consumer society, the constant striving to achieve a decent standard of living placed upon women, the stress involved - life is almost intolerable. Small wonder then that vast numbers of women are so prone to heart disease and nervous exhaustion. Small wonder indeed that the level of divorce is so high.

What can society do to put this right? We should not stop women from working - of course they should work! It is a precious right that has been won at substantial cost. With today's lower birth-rates, society depends on the working woman to function. Just think where the NHS would be without female nurses and doctors! But society needs to understand that although the woman's role has altered and what she still needs is positive, real, substantial help. For instance, whilst society needs an army of working women to function and women need to work to contribute to the household budget in an increasingly expensive world, there is still inadequate provision of that most essential item, childcare facilities. There simply aren't enough places to meet demand and when they are available they are so expensive they can eat up so much of a working mother's income that it hardly seems worthwhile.

No wonder the pressure builds up and has to blow. What blows of course is the marriage.

What else could be done to help? Much has changed in the way men contribute to their families. But many still need constant encouragement to look after the children and the upkeep of the home, to no longer regard themselves as having 'done their bit' by earning the wages. Homemaking is no longer the exclusive preserve of women. Paternity leave is more common and the concept of the house-husband now accepted, although it by far from the norm. Couples should sit down and discuss their domestic roles on a joint, not single basis. It should not automatically be assumed that the burden of running a home and family should fall to the woman.

Keeping a marriage together makes financial sense quite apart from the benefit this would bring to each individual family unit and above all to the children. Today's society has altered beyond all recognition from the accepted values and standards of twenty or thirty years ago. We should consider how to adjust our attitudes accordingly. Happier wives and mothers who are also able to contribute their bit to the national economy would be an advantage to all of us.

5. When love dies

When eight out of ten husbands and seven out of ten wives claim they will never regret their choice of partner, why do so many marriages fail? What happens to these happy partnerships that ultimately leads so many to the divorce courts? Statistically, it is adultery that proves the undoing of most failed marriages, but many would argue that in a genuinely satisfying relationship neither partner would feel the need to stray in the first place.

If adultery is the symptom, what is the root cause? The answer, in a word, is boredom. It creeps up unnoticed, making everything within the marriage seem lacklustre and everything outside the marriage exciting. It starts off as complacency, develops into resentment and finally leads to contempt. Although few husbands or wives would seek a divorce on the grounds of boredom alone, the problem is that the slow advance of boredom makes it difficult to recognise until much of the damage is done, when complacency has led to carelessness. In many cases, this carelessness reveals itself in the form of apathy towards one's partner. And if that partner is feeling neglected, a chance compliment from someone else can trigger off emotions that threaten the marriage. In a situation like this, it is all too easy to wonder whether there is any point in resisting temptation. The earth no longer moves inside the marriage, there's an exciting new world out there and if no-one finds out, what's the harm in it anyway?

It is unrealistic to expect to be able to maintain the romantic intensity of the wedding day for the rest of your married life. Marriage matures in the same way that people do, and many would say that maturity is a great deal more satisfying than the often shallow excitement of youth. The thing to ask yourself is whether you are prepared to give up true companionship and understanding for a fleeting , if passionate, fling. It may well do wonders for the ego but the price to pay may become out of all proportion to the pleasure gained. Because even though it may have got a bit muddled over the years, companionship and understanding is what most married couples do have and what they value.

In a survey on relationships, loyalty, affection and humour come way on top when husbands and wives were asked about the qualities that mattered most. Physical attractiveness and sexual responsiveness are often way down the list for both men and women. These same surveys invariably show that what really annoys or upsets men and women most is being taken for granted.

The skill is to remain interested in one another and, above all, to show your partner that you do actually care. Some changes might be necessary if your marriage is already showing signs of falling victim to tedium. Try spending more time together or developing new interests that you can share. Remember when you first began dating how you would make that special effort with your appearance, how you would surprise each other with little gifts. Just because a relationship is long standing is no excuse to stop trying.

I know a man who has been married to the same woman for 35 years and he still says he gets a sense of excitement just meeting his wife for morning coffee or watching her dress for dinner at a restaurant. The thing to remember is that apathy and complacency breed on themselves. If you are feeling bored and frustrated, it's a safe bet that your partner is feeling the same way too. A good relationship has to be worked on. One of the best pieces of advice I ever heard was by the father of a bride at her wedding reception. In his speech, he advised his daughter and her new husband to always put their partner's happiness above their own. In that way, they would both be happy.

6. Happy holidays!!

The holiday period is one of the rare occasions when the family actually gathers together and spends more than a couple of hours in the same place. Instead of fleeting meetings at the breakfast table, the family is thrust into the unnatural situation of having to relax, play, eat and drink in each other's company for days on end. For most, of course, the friction created by this unusual state of affairs is a minor obstacle to be negotiated in the pursuit of pleasure: everyone is going to enjoy themselves whether they like it or not. There are others, though, who find the fortnight that the British now insist on spending with the family over Christmas more than their marriage can stand. The only other occasion when the family lives together like this is the summer holiday and, sadly, it is no coincidence that divorce lawyers are often at their busiest in January and September.

What is it about these times of the year that can have such a devastating effect on marriages that seem to survive the rest of the year with relative ease? Ask the mum who is struggling to defrost a 10 lb turkey on Christmas morning as the kids complain that there are no batteries in their walking, talking Bart Simpson doll, and you are not going to have to wait long for an answer. Look at the business man in your local wine bar who spends Christmas Eve lunchtime letching after young secretaries with mistletoe and tinsel in their hair. It isn't hard to imagine the reception he'll get when he staggers hone with incriminating lipstick stains on his collar. Or consider the couple that are already finding it hard to make ends meet, and then are subjected to the most intense pressure from friends, children and advertisers to spend, spend, spend.

The trouble with all these explanations is that they are too simple. Like it or not, they have gradually become part of Christmas today, and are unlikely to be grounds for divorce in reality anyway. All three examples, however, are symptomatic of the pressure that exists at particular times of year to 'enjoy' the occasion come what may, to have everything just right on the big day itself. The reality rarely lives up to the dream; just as Santa isn't going to deliver every single present that a child has asked for, the dinner isn't all going to be ready on time and the video is going to go on the blink just before the special edition of "Only Fools and Horses'.

The vast majority of families accept these disasters as part and parcel of the whole process of 'having fun together'. But there are a few who find that it is all too much and they are pushed over the edge. And therein lies the real answer.

If a marriage founders over Christmas, the chances are that it was on pretty rocky ground beforehand. It is hard enough for any marriage to cope with the extraordinary combination of circumstances that creates stress and friction over the festive season. Some of these are financial pressures, worrying about how to cope when the credit card bills start dropping through the door in the New Year. Too much alcohol can loosen the tongue and heighten the tensions. When a marriage is already teetering on the brink of collapse, it is little wonder that this intensely emotional period can prove to be the final straw.

The thing to remember is that if your marriage can survive Christmas, it can survive anything. So don't cry out for a divorce on December 26 because the chances are that if you were fine before Christmas, you'll be fine again by the New Year. Get it in perspective. And you'll have a whole six months in which to really enjoy yourself before having to tackle the horrors of the family summer holiday!

7. Love the second time around

Of course, marital problems are not only confined to the young and lovestruck. I recently came across a fascinating statistic which threw a new light on the rising numbers of couples in their 50s who are getting divorced at a time when they should be celebrating their silver wedding anniversaries. Indeed, it should perhaps make us look again at the whole concept of marriage in the 21 st century. The statistic concerned was not about marriage at all, but rather about life expectancy in a particular third world country. Latest figures showed that over the last 10 years, the average lifespan for a woman in this country had risen from 45 to 58 and for a man from 43 to 57.

It was a sobering statistic. At a time when millions of people around the world are reaching the end of their natural life, thousands of couples in this country are embarking on a new life in a second marriage and can reasonably expect to spend almost as long with their new partner as the entire lifespan of many third world people

I believe these simple statistics point up some larger questions. Was marriage ever meant to last forever in the context of increasing life expectancy in the West? If not, should we be at all shocked by the rising numbers of divorces? And what right does any government have to legislate to force adults who don't want to be together to stay married? The latest official statistics also confirm this trend. The mean age for divorce continues to rise. In 2000 the average age for a man to divorce was 41.3 years and for a woman, 38.8. And there seems to be two distinct reactions among women involved; those with independent financial means and a career often look forward with eager anticipation to a new life whilst those women who have devoted their entire being to the family and find themselves suddenly abandoned see only a future of fear, loneliness and poverty.

There are a number of reasons to explain this latest social trend. Rising numbers of men retiring early or being made redundant in their 50's mean couples being forced for the first time in their relationship to spend a lot of time together and discovering they actually don't like each other that much. Changing social attitudes to divorce mean that couples in this situation are more likely than before to seek a way out of their marriage. Couples who forged their attitudes towards marriage in the liberal 60's were less likely than previous generations to feel they had to stay together once their children had grown up. And then there is the increasing financial independence of women when even wives without paid employment realise they can have some financial independence because of new pensions-sharing legislation.

A striking feature of the trend is the different outcomes for men and women. Men are far more likely to have a new partner after divorce than women, something more pronounced with advancing age. By the age of 65 there are about 125 divorced women to every 100 divorced men according to the National Office of Statistics. Taken together with the fact that women live longer, there is likely to be an increase in the number of elderly women living alone. The words 'till death us do part' may have been entirely appropriate for an earlier age when people married later and lived for far fewer years. Can they really be said with conviction today?

8. Changing aspirations

The majority of divorces in the UK are instigated by women. They either stem from their husband's adultery or violence, the realisation that the person she now wakes up next to in a morning is no longer the man she married or because she has come to accept that she married the wrong person to begin with. There is another cause of divorce, though, which has become increasingly common as the aspirations of women have changed.

This happens when a wife's work environment becomes far more stimulating and more rewarding than that of her husband's. Eventually her values change and her aspirations develop to such an extent that her husband is left trailing in her wake. It can happen in all walks of life and to all types of people. It can happen to newly-weds just starting out in their careers and it can happen to couples who have been married for many years. It can happen to women who have always worked and it can happen to mothers returning to work once the children are out from under their feet. And because the British economy depends on women making up a larger proportion of the workforce during the coming decade, more women are going to rise to senior positions, and the syndrome will gradually affect more and more marriages.

Consider this example. A couple marry in their late teens or early twenties. He is a semi-skilled apprentice and she has a secretarial job with an insurance company. They share the same interests, and outside of work spend their lives together socialising with the same friends. Five years later, things have changed dramatically, for her at least. Although he has now served his apprenticeship he still does basically the same job. His 'Jack-the-Lad' happy to go out for a beer with the boys approach to life, no longer seems so amusing to her. He works with the same people and his outlook on life has not changed one iota: pay the bills and spend whatever is left on a good time.

She, on the other hand, has progressed from making tea and sorting the post to far more responsible duties. She is highly competent with computers, has learnt how to design the boss's powerpoint presentation and has moved up to be a Personal Assistant to a senior director. She is organising business lunches, she is invited to receptions and possibly she is even travelling extensively on business.

Through the dynamic environment into which she has unconsciously been drawn, her view of life and what it can hold has changed beyond recognition. A few drinks every Friday and a fortnight on the Costa del Sol every August are no longer enough. She wants to move up in the world and he doesn't. The result, unless they work incredibly hard to overcome these major differences will inevitably be bitterness and envy, and ultimately the breakdown of the marriage.

Most people already know a couple like this, and wonder 'What is she doing with him?' The thing is, it's not his fault. It's not her fault either. When they met they were entirely compatible, but she has been taken away from their original lifestyle by a totally different working environment.

Luck, as in every other aspect of life, can play its part. None of us at 40 are the people we were at 20. If we are lucky we will have grown closer to our partner, our personalities and expectations of life running in harmony; if we are unlucky we will, through no conscious choice, have fallen apart on life's trials and tribulations, two individuals sharing a bed and a surname and little else.

That there isn't really a similar 'male syndrome' to speak of is a reflection on woman's traditional role in society. It is expected that a woman will grow and develop her lifestyle in parallel with that of her husband. There must be very few women who find it hard to come to terms with, and adapt to, a successful husband (although I have met many such husbands who would not agree). But reverse the roles and many men are unable to cope. Is it that men are generally more insecure? Or are they less able to adapt? Or is it that women are simply more sensible in welcoming their partner's success?

9. Can the law keep pace with lifestyle changes

The cosy and traditional picture of the family, mother, father and two children in their quiet suburban semi, has long been an outdated concept. Changes in social attitudes, greater equality and opportunity for women and evolving work patterns have all contributed to creating a greater diversity of relationships than ever before. Just look at how the most popular soaps on television now depict everyday life and love – transexual Hayley and husband Roy in Coronation Street, the gay GP Dr. Fonseca in Eastenders, gay boy living with straight girl and her baby in Emmerdale. The phrase ' human melting pot' was originally coined to describe the rainbow coalition of races that make up the population of New York, but it could equally be used to describe the miasma of human relationships in Britain today.

But in this new century those changes will seem tame. Continuing medical advances coupled with the cult of individual rights and an almost anything goes attitude to sexual relations mean that we will see change on an unprecedented scale. And the question is: Can the laws which govern family relationships and how we deal with each other as responsible human beings, keep pace.

Just consider some recent developments. Two openly, homosexual British millionaire businessmen get the family they cannot possibly physically produce themselves by using a surrogate mother in California and sperm from one of the men. In America they win a landmark legal victory to have their names recorded as parents on the birth certificates of month old twin girls, a ruling that Britain does not recognise. Is the very fact that two men are allowed to create a family in this way a liberating example of the freedom of the individual or a bizarre and offensive aberration of the natural pattern of human life? There are powerful views both ways.

Then there was the reported case of the grieving parents who are threatening legal action to be allowed to use the frozen sperm of their dead son to create a grandchild. Is this the understandable longing of a bereaved couple to remember their much loved son or a self-indulgent attempt at playing God by creating life after death?

Dame Justice Butler Sloss, the highest ranking woman judge in the country and who, ever since she chaired the difficult and painful Cleveland Child Abuse inquiry has been seen as a champion of children's rights, says that she sees nothing wrong with the principle of adoption by same-sex couples. Sensible acknowledgement that what matters most to a child is a loving and caring home or capitulation to trendy, modern views about gay and lesbian relationships?

There are now proposals to introduce new legislation that will give gay partners and unmarried couples similar rights as those who are married. The bill proposes the creation of 'civil partnerships.' On top of all this comes news that scientists have made a breakthrough in the development of artificial sperm making it technically possible for two women to have a baby without the involvement of a man at all!

All these permutations on the make-up of the family unit are as a direct result of advances in medical techniques and changes in social attitudes. Yet they may only be the foretaste of more to come. The provisions of the Human Rights Act are all-embracing and whilst doing great things for the rights of the individual, they will, without doubt, create the opportunity for endless litigation by people pursuing what they believe to be their rights in the area of the family, the 'right' to have children and to form relationships of their choosing.

We are facing a period of massive change in the legal status of relationships where anything and everything seems possible. As so often, we can look to America for a lead in where we may be heading. It's there that one State now recognises the right of same sex couples to marry and where the courts recently permitted two homosexual men to be legally registered as the parents to two babies produced by surrogate birth. At a time when the Church seems to have less importance in the lives of many people, where do we turn for guidance in creating the new forms of family? It will undoubtedly be the courts that are called upon to set out these conditions based on the concept of human rights. Not everyone will be comfortable with the changes coming our way. The only certainty is that they will come. The roller-coaster is unstoppable.

PART II

Now that
it's Over

10. Facing the facts

If it comes to it and divorce is the only available option how do you deal with the fact? I think there is only one way. Take it right on the chin. Life is made up of happy events and unpleasant events. How we cope with them, how we come through them, determines our personality and our character. In fact if I were a philosopher instead of a lawyer I would propound a view that life is made up of a series of tests. It is how you deal with each test that determines the kind of individual you are.

Frankly, I don't encourage those clients who exhibit only the negative emotions. Not all lawyers take a ' hands on approach' with these clients but I do. It is healthy to cry of course. It is healthy to be distressed but those who seek to hide their emotions are damaging themselves in the long term. In fact I have a regular supply of tissues in my own office because it is quite normal for clients to become extremely upset at the beginning of a case. When a client first comes to see me, it is no surprise-indeed it is expected -for the client to break down in tears. Their emotions are at their rawest; the pain at its most intense. People suffer from depression, misery and compulsive behaviour such as drinking or even stealing. Many people will lose weight, some gain weight. Often they may suffer from sleeplessness, rashes, aches and pains, the causes of which are not physical. Coupled with the stress of marital breakdown, they also have to contend with wholesale gossip with 'friends' who have turned into town criers overnight. Small wonder, then, that in the initial stages of a divorce clients are overwrought and emotionally stressed to the limit.

What I find very hard to deal with, is the client who persists on concentrating on the negative rather than the positive. If something has happened then it has to be faced. The future is all important, not the past. Tomorrow can be affected; yesterday can't be changed. The questions of who, why, how could this happen, etc., are all very well in the short term but in the long term they are positively harmful. The gossips will soon move on to pick over the bones of the next meaty story. Your husband may have formed a new relationship – he is not coming back.

The best remedy is to concentrate on the future. Leave your marital problems with your lawyer, after all that's what you're paying him or her for. Force yourself to do other things and think of other things. Stop texting and waiting for replies that don't come. Feelings of revenge, bitterness, anger and depression are all very well but they destroy only the person who feels them and have no apparent effect on the target of those emotions. Some clients can spend a long time feeling sorry for themselves, wallowing in self-pity, but that is not the answer, harsh and hard though this may seem at the time.

The required approach is one of confidence in oneself and in the future, however daunting that future may appear. If we all were aware of what was going to happen to us in the future there would not be much point in living, but we do live, tomorrow does come. Given time and the right attitude- a positive and patient attitude-people come through divorce stronger and more self-sufficient than they ever were. It simply takes the right attitude.

11. So you've finally had enough

So you've weighed up the situation, assessed the pros and cons and made the decision to divorce. Congratulations. You have taken control of the situation and taken the first step on the road to the rest of your life. So what next?

The first thing is to instruct your solicitor. If you don't have one, find one. At times like this, when your emotions are in turmoil, this can seem an additional, unwanted burden. Where do you start? What should you look for in a solicitor? How can you tell a good lawyer from a bad one? Most people tend to look to a friend or a relative for advice. Perhaps someone close who has been through the divorce process themselves. Don't worry, this problem has been recognised and action taken to make it easier and simpler for you to make the right and appropriate choice.

The Law Society, the governing body for solicitors, has created the Family Law Panel to operate a two tier system of accreditation for those lawyers working in the complex area of divorce and family law. Members have to pass a rigorous test of their professional ability and they are then permitted to use the scheme's blue, 'Family Lawyer' logo on their stationary and as a sign outside their offices. This distinctive logo is your assurance that the lawyer using it has been judged by their peers to be a competent and caring professional. Around 3,600 lawyers in the UK have so far been accredited to the scheme and they are working day in and day out in almost every town and city across the country. I was proud and privileged to be appointed Chief Examiner and Chief Assessor of the Panel. The simple question we asked ourselves when assessing candidates on the first tier was: 'Would we be happy to recommend them to a friend or relative about to go through a divorce?' At specialist level, the process is even more rigorous and the standard very high.'

I believe we have a very high standard of family lawyer in this country but I also believe that the work of the Family Law Panel is helping to raise those professional standards even higher. The ultimate beneficiary is the public.

Theoretically a divorce will take about 12 to 16 weeks from start to finish. I emphasise the 'theoretical'. And there can be good reason to delay. It helps to protect spousal benefits in the event of death before a final order is made.

The procedure is straightforward and basic. In fact, a couple with no financial problems and who are in agreement could easily obtain a divorce without the assistance of a solicitor although I would always advise obtaining legal advice to be absolutely sure nothing has been missed.

It is fashionable to criticise the high rate of divorce and seek to find methods of keeping families together. There are obvious socioeconomic reasons for this, the most basic being the reduced cost to the state and - a fact which cannot be ignored - that it is much easier to keep one family in one home on a certain income level than it is to keep two families in two homes on the same income level. But is actually making the divorce procedure harder the right way? I have my doubts. It is fashionable to express views that divorce should be harder but as a practitioner working daily in that field, and not sitting in an ivory tower pontificating over statistics instead considering the effects on real human beings, I cannot agree. People come to see me when they are so desperate they cannot take anymore. No-one comes to see a divorce lawyer because he or she wants to spend money with them. There are many other , much more enjoyable ways of spending money.

An immediate divorce, as we will see, is to find that the marriage has irretrievably broken down as a result of fault, and I am not a fan of this system. To some extent I would prefer a system of divorce on demand without the necessity of fault because as it works in reality the 'fault' which is very often the basis of the petition is so trivial that it appears to turn the whole procedure itself into a farce. As I have indicated earlier, the reason for this is that it is foolish to hold together a marriage which has quite clearly and irretrievably broken down. Therefore people use the system in a way that I am quite sure was never intended. Examples of 'fault' sufficient to obtain a divorce at present can include: the male partner spending all his spare time fishing, drinking excessively and swearing; either partner not showing enough attention or emotion to the other; failing to buy birthday and Christmas presents and refusing to make love.

I do advocate divorce reform but on a sensible basis, on the assumption that people are intelligent and do not willingly obtain a divorce just for the sake of it. I have never had a client like that yet and I think it is very unlikely I ever will. I do not believe that the state is there to spoonfeed and protect a human being from him- or herself. I am all for the rights of the individual as opposed to the financial good of the government in power.

12. The practical steps

Divorce in England and Wales is currently granted on the basis of irretrievable breakdown of marriage. There are currently five 'grounds' which can be used to justify the term 'irretrievable breakdown.'. These are adultery, unreasonable behaviour, desertion, two years separation with consent or five years separation without consent. Although divorces on the last three grounds are not uncommon, in reality the majority of divorces are on the grounds of unreasonable behaviour or adultery. Both of these two grounds offer a speedier route to divorce and when a marriage does break down it is not too difficult to find some instances of unreasonable behaviour.

It is important at the outset to understand that the reason for the divorce has, in the vast majority of cases, no impact on the other two major issues to be resolved – the financial settlement and the question of residence or contact with the children of the marriage.

There are, in practice, six milestones along the route to divorce. Without going into complex legal explanations, it is worth understanding the process.

1. The initial step is to lodge the divorce petition with the court. The person issuing the divorce is called ' The Petitioner' If there are children to the marriage then the petition must be accompanied by a Statement of the Arrangements for Children. The court will then send a copy of the petition to the other partner, ' The Respondent.'

2. The respondent has to complete an Acknowledgement of Service document and indicate whether he or she intends to defend the divorce. The respondent has seven days to reply and at this stage should consult a solicitor, if they have not already done so.

3. When the Acknowledgement of Service is returned – and the majority of divorces in this country are undefended – a copy is sent to the petitioner or

their lawyer. They then have to file an affadavit confirming the details of the divorce petition are correct. Once the affadavit is sworn it is returned to the court which then considers the evidence.

4. Once the affidavit has been received, it is placed before a District Judge. If he or she decides that the documentation is in order a certificate will be granted and sent to the petitioner giving a date when the decree nisi will be pronounced.

5. The decree nisi will be announced in court on the date indicated in the certificate. It is not necessary for anyone to be in court on this occasion.

6. Six weeks after the decree nisi has been issued, the petitioner can apply for the decree to be made absolute. It is important to recognise that the decree nisi does not end the marriage. In order to remarry the decree absolute must be obtained. The delay of six weeks is mandatory and can be shortened only in extreme circumstances. A copy of the decree absolute is sent to both parties. Many people delay obtaining the decree absolute until a financial settlement is in place. This may be a wise course and a check should be made with your solicitor. You should also consider making a will and establishing the basis of ownership of all property with your solicitor. He or she will advise you in more detail based on your individual circumstances.

13. Too late for talking

So you've finally plucked up the courage to end your marriage. You've had enough of the lies, the betrayal and the womanising. You've endured more mental anguish than you ever thought possible, you've cried yourself to sleep on so many nights you've lost count and the strain of trying to put a brave face on it all for the sake of the children and the neighbours has all become too much. You've asked around among your divorced and separated friends for the name of a good lawyer to make sure you get everything you're entitled to. Now you're sat across the desk from this very earnest, sympathetically smiling solicitor who proceeds to drop a bombshell:

" Have you," he says, tentatively, " ever thought about mediation!"If so, then your initial reaction could probably be taken from this brief selection:-

• Isn't that something the United Nations does?
• The time for talking is long gone.
• I don't want to mediate. I don't even want to speak to the b******. I want you, my lawyer, to do the talking and get me the best possible deal to end this nightmare of a relationship.

None of these are the kind of responses anticipated when the last Conservative Government decided to introduce the concept of mediation in the now, largely discredited Family Law Act. Mediation was not intended as a way to attempt to save a failing marriage. Rather, the aim was that it should be a way of ending a marriage that was less acrimonious, less expensive and less demanding of court time. Mediation by professionally trained experts, usually either solicitors or social workers, was seen as a more civilised approach for the 21st century. I embraced the concept enthusiastically, if with a degree of scepticism. I invested some £10,000 to bring over one of the leading experts on mediation from the United States to train all the solicitors in my firm. We were one of the first firms in the country to do this. Then we waited for the floodgates to open. We are still waiting. As a firm we handle thousands of divorce cases each year and I can literally count on the fingers of one hand the number of cases who have opted for mediation. We are a typical, big city law firm. I have no reason to believe that our experience on mediation is any different from other firms around the country. So why the apparent failure of a well intentioned initiative? It's worth looking at the background.

It was largely the rising costs of divorce on the State that led to the last Conservative government formulating the Family Law Act 1996. The aim was to try and reduce this increasing financial drain on the Exchequer and to cut the number of cases going to court. It has only been partially implemented by Lord Irvine, the current Lord Chancellor. Part of the Act introducing the concept of publicly funded mediation was brought in during 1997. It ruled that anyone seeking Legal Aid for their divorce must first attend a meeting to see if their case is suitable for mediation. If it is, they then sit down with a professional and independent mediator to discuss and agree how their finances, property and children are to be dealt with, without their respective lawyers slugging it out.

It sounds fine. Sensible! Rational! Civilised!. Only it's not working. The theory is not translating into action. From personal experience, whenever I mention the option of mediation to my clients the answer is, invariably, no. Their view is that they have come to me to sort it out, they don't want to involve someone else. What these fine theories do not take into account is the emotion of the situation. It is very rare that a couple reach a mutually amicable decision to split. There is inevitably going to be argument about money, houses and children. By the time a client is sat in front of me, they are almost beyond having reasonable discussions with their partner. They just want it over. They have lost confidence in themselves, they are nervous and don't feel qualified to sort it all out. That's why they depend on their lawyer.

If just one partner shows interest in mediation, it is usually the husband, particularly if he is the dominant one in the relationship. He will tend to think that if he can just get his wife on her own, he will be able to talk her round to a settlement on his terms. No, mediation is never going to be the universal panacea that many of its supporters first thought. It will only ever be useful in a minority of cases. Research backs this up. According to the Family Law Mediation Pilot Project, which is run by the Legal Services Commission, there are around 3,000 people a month attending those initial meetings to discover if their cases are suitable for mediation. However, only around 20% of them, some 7-8,000 a year actually go on to use mediation to arrange the end of their marriage, with no guarantee of success and delay in settlement can result. This should be contrasted with the new, structured court timetable and the active participation of judges at the 'Family Dispute Resolution' hearing, which is a success.

I am afraid that by the time a wife has made the decision that things are so bad she needs to see me, or any of the other divorce lawyers in the country, then mediation is the last word she wants to hear. But I don't rule it out later down the line. By then, a solicitor will have obtained disclosure of the side's financial position. At that stage, the imbalance will be redressed. With good legal advice to depend on, in financial matters mediators can be a good thing. As it is put forward now, it is simply too early in the process.

PART III

Now that it's Over

14 Need acrimony follow matrimony?

Men and women respond to divorce differently. For women, the ending of a marriage can be the spark that kindles a whole new life. They find it easier to take stock, to look at themselves and their routines and, after coming to terms with the pain and sense of betrayal, will move on. According to psychologists, most women become far more assertive after divorce and vow never to be so dependent again. The majority of all divorces are initiated by the woman and it is the man who finds it harder to start again when his support system disappears. It's not surprising, therefore, that only half of the women who divorce will re-marry, compared to three-quarters of the men.

Instead of viewing a separation as a failed marriage, it is more positive to see it as the end of a relationship which has run its course. Because many partners do manage to remain friends, it can be a change of relationship rather than a loss. The actual process of divorce is where the potential for bitterness and trauma lies, but most women - once the deciding and dividing is over - do not regret parting. Unfortunately, the law can force a couple to hate each other, no matter how initially friendly their separation. Thankfully, the alternative to matrimony doesn't have to be acrimony. The initial stages may leave room for distrust, but it is possible to treat divorce as a civilised way out of an unsatisfactory partnership. Once the cause of the problems has been removed, such as money disagreements, irritating habits or infidelity, isn't it just possible that you could still like the person who is left?

The persistent worry for many couples is the thought that the happiness of their children would have to be sacrificed for their happy divorce. No-one would willingly put a child through the hurt of seeing a parent leave but who would willingly bring up a child in an atmosphere of constant war? So much depends on individual circumstances.

For anyone contemplating divorce, it's time to sit back and take a long look at the pros and cons - perhaps with the help of a close friend, a GP or counsellor. But the decision rests on whether you picture yourself happier out of the marriage or in it. If you know, without a doubt, that you can't make another go of it, then a positive attitude to divorce will guide you in those first steps towards a new life.

15. The hurt of false hope

Whatever the legal steps towards divorce, in human and emotional terms, cases can basically be divided up into three categories: amicable, acrimonious and agonising.

The first, in which both parties agree that their relationship has run its full course, is probably the easiest. The second, in which one partner has treated the other so badly that reconciliation is simply not worthy of consideration, can be the nastiest but is still relatively clean cut. The third is the saddest of all. In this category, one partner wants a divorce and the other doesn't. She (it is usually the woman) refuses point blank to accept that the marriage is over, and puts up every possible obstacle to the divorce taking place. She does it either out or sheer bloody-mindedness, or because she still harbours the vain hope that they will get back together again, even to the point of ignoring the pile of soilcitor's letters that has built up under the letterbox.

This ostrich-like approach, while perhaps understandable from purely an emotional point of view, can be very expensive in terms of both health and finance. Years of constant stress and turmoil caused by denying the reality of the situation can take its toll on even the fittest and most well-balanced of people, and a nervous breakdown can be the end result. Financially, it can be just as costly.

Marriage is a partnership between two people, hopefully for life but unfortunately not always so. If one partner is set on dissolving the relationship, there is little point in the other trying to keep it going indefinitely. Someone has to help him or her to face reality, snap out of it and accept that the partnership is over. It could be a friend or a member of the family who has to take on this unpleasant task, but often they are too close and the job falls on the shoulders of the solicitor. Counselling is an important part of a solicitor's job, as is full discussion of the likelihood of reconciliation. An experienced solicitor, one who is dealing with divorce work every day of the week, can recognise very quickly whether the possibility of reconciliation actually does exist or, to put it bluntly, whether the client is in reality chasing an impossible dream. When the latter is the case, there is no point in beating about the bush. It helps no-one, least of all the poor wife (or occasionally, yes, the husband) who is sitting there close to breaking point, still carrying false hopes for a partner who has clearly made his or her mind up long ago. To get the message through to a client can involve some hard talking, sometimes even an approach that borders on shock treatment. But it is the only way to help a client out of his or her nightmare as quickly as possible.

In a way, divorce can be compared with bereavement. The body has to be buried before one can even begin to think about getting over a death; similarly divorce is actually a way of breaking with the past. The main difference is that society will support and comfort a bereaved person, whilst sometimes shunning a divorced person as if he or she has done something wrong.

In surveys of situations that cause the most stress to people, divorce regularly comes second only to the death of a spouse. It is my conviction, however, that it is not the divorce itself that is most stressful but the period of pain that precedes it. The actual divorce can be an unburdening, a relief and a new beginning. Once a marriage is over, it is better to reach this point sooner rather than later so that you can pick up pieces, repair your confidence and move on to a life beyond. And if it takes a few home truths to get there, so be it.

PART IV

The Financials

16. It's the money, honey

It is not often that both parties to a marriage will have the same amount of money. If they both had the same amount of income and capital, and neither had any debts, then many of the problems in achieving a suitable financial settlement would be solved. The usual position is that one party has more than the other in terms of both savings and income and usually the person with more is the husband and the person with less is the wife. Usually, also, the wife has the children. Often there are overdrafts, tax liabilities and credit card debts. The divorce court has the problem of sorting out how much of the net savings and income goes to which party. So it can be seen that in the majority of such cases in financial terms the husbands are the 'haves' and the wives are the 'have nots'.

Money can often prove to be a very potent weapon for the person who has it and is in the short term able to buy, for example, immediate representation rather than waiting for Legal Aid, or to reduce maintenance in order to put pressure on the other side. At the end of the day, however, the person with the money is the one who gives and the person without is the recipient. It is little wonder then that such a situation can immediately make for all-out war.

There is an obligation on both parties to be honest and make a full disclosure of their wealth. In practice it is rare that there is a complete disclosure of a person's financial position. More common is partial disclosure, with policies or building society accounts or other assets conveniently slipping by. And it is not just people of modest means who go to great lengths to keep the financial status secret from their spouses. I have dealt with many cases where forensic financial investigations have turned up hidden, off-shore accounts containing millions of pounds that the wife didn't know about. Failure to disclose assets is usually the reason why most legal costs are incurred. The pursuit of assets can incur extremely high costs especially when accountants, actuaries and pension specialists get involved (all of whom are able to send bills) - as well as barristers, at breathtaking charge-out rates.

An important point to remember about a financial settlement is that it can be tailored specifically for each couple's needs. It does not have to follow a set pattern. There are all sorts of permutations that can be used in order to achieve a realistic settlement. Payments of capital, ie. lump sum payments, can be paid part now, part later. Income can be varied or fixed. The Child Support Agency is there to ensure payment of agreed maintenance for children. (This is dealt with in detail in a later chapter).

An agreement can be reached about the split of a pension, redundancy pay, or property to be sold in the future. The watchword is that settlements can be totally flexible. Forget the bar room talk that the house is split fifty-fifty and that the wife will not be entitled to maintenance if she works or if the children are above a certain age. It does not work that way and again the watchword is what is reasonable to both parties. Of course what is reasonable to one might not be reasonable to the other and that is why at the end of the day the courts are left to decide.

Apart from reform of the divorce procedure itself, I would like to see more emphasis on negotiation rather than adversarial confrontation, that it should be a requirement before a case comes to court. New procedures now mean the courts lay down very strict timetables to ensure that all parties keep to agreed dates and avoid unnecessary delay. The court takes a much more hands on approach and will hold a hearing to set technical directions followed by a second at which the judge can determine if the parties are in a position to settle. Only if the case is not settled at this stage will it go to trial and in my personal experience 95% of cases are resolved before that step is taken.

17. Does he have hidden assets?

There was a time when a man's income was his own private affair. Come Friday evening he'd hand over the housekeeping and that was as near as you got to seeing his wage packet. What was left was for him to know and you to only guess at. Surely, though, in the enlightened, liberated 21st Century such secrecy over earnings is a thing of the past. You know precisely what your partner earns, don't you?

While this may often be the case, it is by no means always so. Shares, for instance, may be registered in one name only. Offshore trusts can offer very attractive returns. And if your husband has his own business, estimating his profits could be an extremely complicated affair. While not knowing his full value might seem of little real consequence today, if the unthinkable should happen and he should run off with the next door neighbour, your incomplete knowledge of his financial wheeling and dealing could prove very costly indeed.

In theory, both parties involved in a divorce are legally bound to divulge their assets. In fact, this can be easier said than done. It is not too difficult for anyone with an understanding of basic finance to hide assets away in hard-to-trace accounts. Having a good solicitor on your side significantly raises the chances of unearthing these accounts, but the cost of finding them can take a sizeable chunk out of whatever sum is eventually recovered. This is why I stress the importance of finding out just what your partner is worth before it reaches this stage. Once a divorce gets into full swing, as it were, the atmosphere can and often does turn into one of bitterness and confrontation and your husband may be less than willing to divulge the whereabouts of every last penny.

To many women, this advice might seem somewhat academic. Would that he had the funds and knowledge to stash away secret savings in the first place! Let me give you a couple of examples of wives who thought just that. Neither of them considered that their husbands were anything particularly out of the ordinary when they came to see me, but within a few months the picture had changed completely.

• The first, Nicki, had been married for several years. Her husband Rob ran a small shop selling groceries and, while they were comfortable, there was nothing to indicate that he might have anything hidden away. When Nicki filed for divorce, we carried out a company search just in case. This revealed that in addition to Rob's small corner shop, he also had an extensive portfolio of properties and owned several supermarkets in the area.

• The second case is slightly different in that Louise already felt that her husband Graham might well have one or two 'private' accounts and asked us for our advice. As she hadn't actually told her husband of her intention to divorce him at that point, we suggested that she find out as much as possible about his financial situation before doing so. When the case came to court, Graham declared UK assets of around £100,000. But with the help of Louise's enquiries, we were able to prove the existence of offshore assets running into millions and she received a more than satisfactory settlement.

While these cases are obviously exceptional, they do show the importance of checking every possible avenue before agreeing a settlement. Even if your partner has been with the same firm for twenty or thirty years and could never have built up savings of any real note, he could still be worth a great deal more than you think. There are strict rules about tracing assets and behaving properly. Always ask a solicitor for advice so you cannot be criticised.

At present, this advice might seem relevant only to someone who is considering ending their marriage or is actually in the throes of a divorce. But it is actually aimed more at those people for whom the possibility of divorce currently seems about as likely as discovering that their partner has a numbered bank account in Zurich.

18. Heart and home

When a couple decides that enough is enough and divorce is the only way out, their main priority is usually the welfare of the children. A close second, however, must be where everyone will live after the divorce. Disposing of the family home can be one of the most traumatic aspects of the whole divorce process. You've lived there for years, it holds memories of happier times, yet you are being forced to sell it simply because your partner has fallen for someone else. It hardly seems fair, does it? Yet this is the position that thousands of people find themselves in every year. So what can you do?

First and foremost, you must force yourself to consider the situation as objectively as you can, even under what will undoubtedly be very difficult circumstances. If your husband or wife has found someone else, the chances are that he or she will want to move out to be with the new partner. But if the cause of your divorce is less clear-cut, the longer you can both stay together the better you will be able to plan for, and afford, life apart.

If one of you leaves before the divorce is finalised, which could quite possibly happen, you will have to maintain two properties on an income that was previously dedicated to just one. Even if the plan is eventually to buy two smaller houses, try to make sure that the family home is sold before either of you plunges into the property market or you could be caught out with the impossible burden of indefinite bridging loan repayments.

If staying under the same roof really is out of the question - and very often it will be - you need to make certain that you are both aware of who is going to pay what. If your partner is the main breadwinner and can afford to maintain two homes for the time being and can be relied upon to do so, then fair enough, the arrangements will be to the satisfaction of both of you.

If, however, he moves out full of promises to keep up with the mortgage, and you later discover that you are months in arrears, what can be done? First, let your lender know. Some building societies estimate that up to forty per cent of their arrears are due to divorce or separation, so they understand the problem and will do their best to help. Then contact your solicitor to see whether an order can be obtained to make him pay. If his name is on the mortgage, it will be in his best interests anyway to do so. If the house does eventually have to be repossessed he will be losing money too, and will find it very difficult to obtain another mortgage the future. If he still refuses to pay, and you take over the payments, you will then be able to argue for example that your contributions to the house were such that you are entitled to a larger share when it is eventually sold. Also, if you need to, contact the Benefits Agency for help. They may well be able to assist you. Working Families Tax Credit and assistance in paying the mortgage are areas on which you may need advice and can be very lucrative.

That covers the arrangements prior to divorce, but what of everyone's needs afterwards? Unless you have substantial liquid assets available, selling the family home is often the only way that a couple can afford two properties, but not always.

• An interesting example involves Paul and Julia, who are both in their late thirties. He earns £40k, she earns £10k, they have two children in their early teens and live in a house worth £90,000 with a £30,000 mortgage. Were they to sell the house they would each raise £30,000, ample for Paul to start again, but certainly not enough for Julia and the children. Unfortunately Paul doesn't earn enough to support himself in a new house whilst paying maintenance to his wife and children so they decide to come to a realistic agreement. She accepts his share of the house in full and final settlement and he has to pay no maintenance to her, although he still makes payments to the children. Julia can therefore stay where she is while Paul can afford to start again on the property ladder.

Another example where a person who, under normal circumstances, would be unable to buy out their partner's share but can sometimes retain ownership, involves couples who have been separated for some years. A husband who, after leaving his wife, returns a few years later and demands his share of their joint assets can apply to the court to make an order for sale. However, the time and money that she has put into the property over the intervening years will certainly be taken into account, and she could well be able to extend their mortgage enough to buy out his reduced share. There is also what is known as a Mesher/Martin order. This allows the wife and children to stay in the family house until she remarries or the children reach the age of 17 or such an age as can be agreed between when his agreed shared of the value of the house is payable at that time. This ensures the husband doesn't lose out on the increased value in the property. However, he must beware Capital Gains Tax implications and should talk to his accountant.

Every case depends on the specific income and capital of those involved though, and sadly, more often than not, the house does eventually have to be sold. As unfair as it may seem at the time, the courts are simply not interested in who left whom. Guilt doesn't come into it, the partner who deserted you retains the rights to a share of the assets and, if it comes to it, a court can order you to sell. If that thought does seem unbearable now, think of it this way: a happy small home is infinitely better than an unhappy large home. If it means being able to put a bitter relationship behind you and starting life again free from mortgage, moving house is a small price to pay.

19. Pension planning!

It used to be said that an Englishman's home was his castle and his most important financial asset. These days, however, it's more likely that it's his pension that he guards most jealously, especially when divorce raises the question of sharing the proceeds with his former wife. After negotiations over access to children, those involving allocation of the funds built up in a pension through long years of marriage can be among the most acrimonious and bitter of the whole break up. A husband frequently regards the pension as his reward for a lifetime of work. This is particularly evident in those jobs and careers that demand long and unsociable hours, do not pay excessive salaries but offer generous pension provision at the end. This applies to people working within the civil service and the police, for example.

In these cases, and in many others, the husband will often choose to disregard the fact that it was only the support of his wife that enabled him to work so hard. Caring for their home and children was really her 'contribution' to creating the financial safeguard for their life after retirement. She firmly believes she is entitled to an equitable share. In many cases, after the family home, the pension is the largest financial asset involved in arriving at a settlement. It is a complex and difficult situation.

However, the whole area of pension sharing underwent dramatic change with the introduction of new legislation in 2000. The Welfare Reform and Pensions Act 1999 came into force and had a major impact on financial settlements to the positive benefit of women. So dramatic was it that we saw desperate husbands frantically issuing petitions for divorce in at attempt to have their cases dealt with under the existing, less onerous legislation. At the same time we witnessed equally desperate wives resorting to all sorts of methods to defend and delay petitions in order to preserve their enhanced rights under the new legislation as it will apply only to petitions issued on or after December 2000.

To understand the impact of the new legislation, it's worth recalling the position.

As everyone knows, pensions are complex and confusing and the entire industry has been through a radical shake-up since the pensions mis-selling scandals of the 1990s. Vast numbers of people in this country make no financial provision for their retirement other than relying on the state pension. The pensions industry and the Government is actively trying to change this culture by making people aware that, given the increasing demands on the Exchequer, they are going to have to take a greater degree of financial responsibility for their lives beyond retirement. There are many different kinds of pensions currently available. These include the statutory state schemes, occupational schemes, small self-administered schemes, personal pensions, retirement annuity contracts and the new stakeholder pensions, although the take-up on these has been disappointingly low..

Most people expect to pay into their chosen pension scheme all their working life and for the fund to develop in such a way as to provide for them into their old age. It's just a figure that disappears from the wage packet each month and most people give it no more thought than that, until one of two things happens:-

(i) Retirement is looming and they realise that their pension entitlement is woefully inadequate to sustain their desired lifestyle, particularly as we are living longer.

(ii) The marriage they thought was for life is falling apart and the wife is demanding a share of the pension.

The first task in any negotiations between lawyers representing the parties in a divorce is firstly to establish just what pensions are in existence and then to attempt to value the schemes. The accepted method is to look at the Cash Equivalent Transfer Value. However, projected future benefits must also be considered.

Among other questions to be answered are:-

• Does the scheme offer a lump sum on retirement, pension income, death in service benefits, death benefits after retirement, transfer to other schemes, widows benefits?

• How is that loss to be quantified on divorce? Then there is the question of ensuring that the whole of the benefits are actually disclosed during the negotiations. Additional Voluntary Contributions can sometimes slip through the net; entire schemes have been known to go undiscovered leading to the financial disadvantage of the former wife, eg SERPS.

So, what is the present position?

The most important effect of the legal changes was to allow for pension sharing straightaway. Part of the pension fund (or whatever is agreed or ordered by the court) can be transferred off to the other spouse immediately. This means that both parties can then get on with their lives as the asset that they have been paying into (one directly, the other indirectly) and which continued to bind them together, has been dealt with.

The provisions of the new legislation are having a significant impact on settlements.

The courts will still continue to use their discretion in making settlements, basing judgements on things like reasonable needs, contributions, ages of the parties, length of the marriage, etc are taken into account. A 30-something wife is still unlikely to end up with much, if any, of her husband's pension whilst a 50-something wife, whose husband is, say, a surgeon with little capital but a big pension can certainly expect a good share-out.

There are a number of examples of wives whose husbands have jobs where the income is not high but the real perk is the pension. These women have traditionally been caught up in an injustice when there are no assets to compensate for loss of pension benefits and no way of dividing up the fund. There have been attempts in the past to stop divorce in such cases but it is notoriously difficult; a wife has to be virtually on the poverty line before a court will take this action. There will still be earmarking and there will still be the option of separation rather than divorce. There will still, inevitably, be all the problems associated with valuing the pension as part of the divorce settlement. But the new legislation should, at least, make life easier if the asset can be dealt with at the time rather than having to consider the value based on future projections.

One thing, however, is certain. It amounts to a positive step forward for women.

20. The right settlement for you!

Depending on whether they are the potential payer or recipient, clients always have the million-dollar question they want answering at their first appointment. It is either "How much will I get?" or "How much will it cost me?"

Of course, no solicitor can provide a simple answer to that enquiry. So, in common with lawyers up and down the country, I have a number of stock questions to ask that will enable me to frame my advice. In anticipation that you are going to see a solicitor I suggest you have the following information to hand. It is not an exhaustive list and much will depend on your own particular circumstances. (There is quite a difference between a client of mine "who couldn't manage without at least £5k per month for clothes" and the lady whose expenditure was devoted entirely to maintaining her farm where she had happily spent the last 35 years.)

First your full name and address (It's amazing how many people give this information wrongly). Please make sure that this is your correct correspondence address. Do not overlook the possibility that your spouse will read your correspondence or may even decide to tap the telephone or put a tracker on your car. It happens in practice! Then your date of birth. Ditto in relation to your spouse. Date of marriage. (Some people blank this date out in their memory). Details of jobs. Your respective incomes. (Don't worry if it's only round figures or estimated. At this stage that isn't too important and many people don't have a clue.) Details of properties – address, ownership, mortgage (amount outstanding), type of mortgage (ordinary repayment, endowment, pension linked). Approximate value. If in doubt contact a local estate agent for a rough idea. Properties abroad are more difficult to value. Details of the purchase price will help. Then, details of all the rest of the assets. Details of companies and shareholding. (Don't worry if you only have a vague idea or none at all! This too is common. An experienced solicitor will unearth the position.) Other assets will include money in banks or building societies, monies invested in shares or insurances, pensions (rough values will help) and all other assets such as house contents, cars furniture, jewellery, antiques etc.

It's amazing what material things a couple can amass and how easily the details can be forgotten. I once had a client whose husband "forgot" to mention his plane and the boat berthed in Mallorca. His wife had genuinely forgotten about them as well and originally he had no intention of reminding her - but he did so.

Values are based on a second hand or sale basis, not insurance or replacement cost. Any potential tax liability will be taken into account.

There is a duty of full and frank disclosure between the parties and to the court. Failure to disclose could result in the order being set aside.

Example. James and Davina divorce. James uses a solicitor. Davina, to save costs, does not. James "forgets" to disclose £1million of share options to the court. He tells Davina that because they are only options they are of no current value and therefore irrelevant. She believes him. She settles for a pittance. Three years later she regrets her decision. She is financially desperate. She hires a solicitor, who has the original order set aside and James ends up paying several hundred thousand pounds more and the costs.

Example. Take the case of Sandra and Jim. He is worth millions. He discloses all his assets at the outset. His extremely shrewd solicitor negotiates an agreement with Sandra's far less experienced solicitor for a fraction of what she would obtain in court. She settles. A year later regretting her decision she decides to try and set that order aside. She fails. She has no grounds to do so and ends up paying his costs. She is left trying to sue her first solicitors.

Once there is a summary of the assets and income a solicitor can give an initial estimate as to what the potential outcome may be. At this stage there will be quite a bit of "but if" and "subject to" which every lawyer is very used to saying. You can't expect to hold a lawyer rigidly to his initial opinion which is bound to change as the facts become clearer, but it should be something you can broadly rely on.

A solicitor doesn't guess what a settlement will be. It isn't "weighed" on scales or dreamed up out of thin air. The law is contained in section 22-25 of the Matrimonial Causes Act 1973. It sounds very dry and dusty but I keep a copy in my desk drawer because I need to constantly show it clients to explain how these things work!

The law permits applications for maintenance before and after divorce, various forms of lump sums, property adjustment orders and pension sharing orders. Applications can be made for children, but capital orders for children are rare. The court, in truth, has very wide powers indeed. It can look into trusts whether on or offshore. Orders can be made in relation to foreign property. Only at the most esoteric levels might there be a problem say in relation to a pension sharing order of a foreign pension but that is far from the norm.

The factors to be taken into account by the court are contained in section 25. The court must first consider the welfare of the children as paramount and if a clean break is possible between the parties to do so. This means sufficient capital is paid to end any obligation for maintenance. The court takes into account the needs, obligations and responsibilities of the parties, their contributions (financial and non-financial), their ages, the length of the marriage, any likely alteration in their circumstances and the loss of potential benefits caused by a divorce, such as spousal pensions.

Sometimes behaviour might be relevant but it has to be pretty bad. Adultery on its own is not bad enough to be taken into account. Stabbing your husband in the throat so his voice disappears will definitely affect the settlement! This case was one of the very first divorce cases I ever handled and I don't recommend it! There are far more sensible ways to end a marriage. More common is dreadful behaviour by one party during the proceedings themselves, and this can be penalised in costs.

In the divorce of James and Zoe, nobody was going to tell James what to do. He was far too clever to listen to his wife and her fancy upstart lawyer (me). His first action was to bug every telephone in my client's home. Then he had her arrested 3 times by the police on trumped up charges of fraud and forgery. He launched an application for the children to live with him, to put pressure on the wife, which his own lawyers conceded as soon as it came to court. He hid assets. He produced accounts that were false. He failed to give proper disclosure which meant we had to do all the work to find out his true worth.

Every time he saw me, he stopped his car alongside, swearing and threatening me with his fist. He ran up a bill on both sides of £200k in legal fees. When the case came to court, the judge went to town on him and he was ordered to pay every penny of his wife's costs and his assets were injuncted until she and us had been paid out. In short he paid £400k for nothing. Not so clever after all!!!.

Then what? Here comes the technical bit. Have ready details of your budget needs and those of your spouse as you see it and the children. This will assist your solicitor. Then sit back and listen to the endless possibilities and realise that the bar room talk is wrong; a 50/50 split and off you go to start a new life may not be the answer for you (okay, it may have worked for your best friend who got divorced but she didn't have your problems and her settlement is nothing to do with yours.) By this I mean, your settlement is tailor made for you and is unique to you. What is right for you and yours may not be the same for anyone else. So stop comparing yourself to Ivana Trump!!.

You could have maintenance, a house and some capital. You could have all capital if you want just the cash. You could have a pension share, maintenance for life or until remarriage and a house. You could have maintenance for a term of years and a house. You could have no maintenance for yourself, maintenance for the children, including school fees, and remain in the big house whilst the children are minors. Then it could be sold and the proceeds divided. You could have the house with the mortgage paid off. You could have two houses, the boat, the apartment in the South of France and the pension. In short you could have whatever is fair and reasonable within the context of the assets and section 25 Matrimonial Causes Act 1973. Your own lawyer will advise you further. I won't attempt to try.

Certain cases that have become standards are supposed to have made the job a little easier. Ask the lawyers in the field if they agree. A knowledgeable reference to the landmark judgement given in 2000 of White –v- White (and I keep a copy of that too in my drawer) will sufficiently alarm your lawyer to make sure you get the best possible advise. In that case the House of Lords confirmed a split of assets as to 40/60 in the husband's favour.

The starting point is section 25 of the Matrimonial Causes Act. First the needs of the parties have to be satisfied, then surplus assets should be divided. In most cases there won't be any. However, in the cases of the very wealthy, and where there has been a long marriage, irrespective of whether the wife has worked, 50/50 is the starting point. It won't be the finishing point in most cases. I don't wish to unnecessarily inflate or deflate your hopes. Ask your lawyer as you are paying him or her and not me.

And finally, check your settlement. In the case of Sandra and Nick, had she asked for a second opinion perhaps by insisting on taking a barrister's advice she would never have been in the position she finds herself in today. Make sure tax isn't ignored. There are tax advantages for couples who split assets potentially liable to capital gains tax between themselves during the tax year in which they finally separate, not divorce. The potential liability to capital gains tax could cost a great deal. Ask your lawyer for advice. If the response is vacant staring into space, consider a change! If only Sandra had checked.

21. Maintenance and when he refuses to pay

Rarely has the subject of a father's financial responsibilities to his child – legitimate or otherwise - been more topical than it is today. While fatherhood has made the headlines for Boris Becker and Mick Jagger, it has also highlighted an issue that causes immense problems for women from all walks of life; how best to ensure that the fathers of their child meets his financial obligations once the couple are no longer together..

Child support maintenance is an amount of money that non-resident parents pay regularly as a contribution towards the financial support for their children. Both parents have a legal responsibility to support their children financially if they can afford to do so. As in most cases the children will reside with their mother when the marriage breaks down, it is most often the woman who has to face the issue of exactly who will pay what towards the upbringing of the children.

Before the advent of the Child Support Agency, getting an ex -partner to actually stump up the maintenance that had already been agreed was a tedious process. Every year, around 80,000 mothers in the UK were forced to take a former partner to court over the issue. This was only a proportion of the women who were entitled to apply. Many didn't bother. It was a costly process, both financially and emotionally, and one in which rarely anyone ever really "won". The mother only received what she was entitled to anyway. The father sees it as his ex twisting the knife. And the children, still already in shock from the break up of their parents marriage, see a father who is trying to shirk his responsibility for them.

Maintenance enforcement cost the government nearly £3.3 billion a year and often, women would find themselves in a no win situation. If a former partner was paid in cash, had no assets and kept disappearing, the pragmatic view of the situation was to give up. It would be near impossible to keep tabs on him and his payments. The same advice usually applied if he went abroad. Unless a woman had a substantial amount of capital to invest in chasing him through the foreign courts once you found him, it was simply not worth the time, or effort and expense.

Thankfully, in recent years much has changed. In April 1993 a new system was introduced to combat these problems with the launch of the Child Support Agency. Most new maintenance assessments in respect of children are now dealt with by the CSA instead of the courts, as previously. The system was intended to be more user-friendly, fairer, and make it harder for fathers unwilling to pay the maintenance they owe to get away with it.

In its early stages, the agency was subject to much bad press. Careless investigation and administrative errors caused many children to be poorer and parents to face a bureaucratic nightmare. As time has gone on, things have improved. The legislation has now been further reformed to try to achieve the original objectives. The CSA has increased the number of cases processed in less than 20 weeks from 12,081 in April 2000 to 14,819 in March 2001.Compliance has also improved with an increase in the number of cases fully compliant by 16.% from 159,800 to 185,420, enabling them to increase the amount of child maintenance collected to some £537 million..'

The CSA exists to assess, collect and pay child support maintenance ensuring that parents who live apart meet their financial obligations to their children. Its aim is to deliver an excellent child support service to help reduce child poverty and put children first by ensuring that absent parents are not allowed to shirk their responsibilities. The CSA has powers to order a parent to pay maintenance for a child taking into account a number of factors.

Under the Child Support, Pensions and Social Security Act, 2000, maintenance will, from the start date, be calculated according to a set formula. Fathers will be required to pay 15% of their take home pay for one child, 20% for two and 25% for three. There are amendments for factors where both parents share in the upbringing of the child.

Another issue for consideration is child maintenance from the courts for such items as school fees or for additional expenditure not covered by CSA assessment.

Whatever your particular circumstances, going back to court soon after a divorce, or approaching the Child Support Agency, can seem a daunting prospect, but coping without his money could be a whole lot worse. And that is something you should never lose sight of. Making him pay isn't an act of greed or retribution, it is simply asking him to contribute towards the upbringing of the children that he helped to bring into this world in the first place.

22. Counting the cost

For anyone who has ever been affected by a divorce, whether directly or indirectly, the emotional turmoil is obvious. Multiply this sadness and bitterness by a factor of 140,000 - the number of couples now divorcing every year in the UK - and the emotional cost of this blight on our society reaches immeasurable proportions.

Slightly easier to quantify, but no less staggering for it, is the financial cost. Taking into account the increased burden of single parent families on the social system, the cost of divorce is reckoned to be in the region of an astonishing £3 billion a year, with legal fees accounting for nearly three-quarters of this figure. For those without calculators - that works out at roughly £9,000 per couple, and while the cost of a straightforward divorce is only going to be a fraction of this figure, some people are clearly paying a lot of money in order to untie the matrimonial knot.

So why does divorce cost so much, and what can a couple do to keep the costs down? An expensive divorce (and one celebrity recently paid £2 million to part from her husband!) is caused by one of two things. Either the couple's financial affairs are so complex that a whole team of specialists is required to sort them out, or, more usually, one or the other partner believes it possible to gain something from spinning the whole affair out for as long as possible. A bitter wife might decide to argue out even the most trivial details in court as a way of 'making him suffer'. Or a dishonest businessman might not declare all his worth in the hope that assets remain hidden and undivided. While one can perhaps understand the motives of both, such an approach can and often does backfire. To take the wife's attitude to the extreme, she could eventually find herself with nothing at the end, as all their assets have been eaten up in legal costs. Even if this doesn't happen, the court could ask her to meet her husband's costs as well as her own because of her obstinate, bloody-minded attitude. This shouldn't deter anyone who has a reasonable claim from pressing home his or her case, but it should serve as a warning against 'litigation for the sake of revenge'.

It is here, therefore, in the area of commonsense and compromise, that the most important lesson of economical divorce can be learned. Every additional complication that a solicitor has to investigate or settle inevitably ends up on the bill. While you might believe that the hi-fi system your partner cherishes is worth £200 more than he claims, is it really worth spending £500 to prove the point?

Another important point to consider is whether you might be eligible for Legal Aid . It is not guaranteed to absolve you of all responsibility for your bill! If you do receive or retain an amount of capital as part of your settlement, you could well be asked to repay the Legal Aid fund any of the costs that it has met on your behalf. There is a great deal of misunderstanding about Legal Aid, so while it is extremely helpful in getting your case to court, it is worth knowing what your eventual responsibilities might be. Do not ever assume that Legal Aid means your case will be handled for free. Rather, consider it as a deferred payment scheme with interest clocking up merrily. Remember, there is a rarely any such thing as a free lunch.

So, to the $64,000 - or should it be £3 billion -question: how much is my divorce going to cost me? If you are legally aided, your costs will be much lower. But at the same time, because he or she will be meeting the office overheads, don't expect every fee-earner in the practice or that particular practice at all to do Legal Aid. The poor remuneration rates usually make Legal Aid for some firms a non-starter. In financial terms, the lawyer is usually working for less than quarter of the normal rate to meet even the overheads. How many people can work forever at a loss? Yet many lawyers on the whole do retain a commitment to Legal Aid even if many cannot afford the full-blooded commitment which as philanthropists they would prefer.

If you are a private client, then a great deal depends on where you live. For example, it is by no means unusual for a London-based solicitor, with enormous overheads, to charge anything around £500 an hour, whereas in a major provincial city such as Leeds or Manchester the rate is likely to be somewhere between £75 and £300. This will include a charge for 'care and control' which is roughly proportional to the complexity of the case and the value of the assets in dispute. For instance, a woman claiming a share of assets worth £2 million will probably pay more than a woman claiming a share of £200,000, even if the two cases take the same amount of work. This is because of the value of the service provided. In other words, two hours' work on behalf of the first client might obtain her a million pounds while the same work for the second client might be worth several thousands.. The care and control factor usually represents the solicitor's profit in the case. As a very rough guide to costs (and it cannot be overstressed that every single divorce is different) let's look at three hypothetical cases, based on an average High Street solicitor's chargeout rate.

• Helen and Peter, who have no children, some capital built up in their home but no dispute over what assets they possess could actually do the divorce themselves for nothing by filling out the relevant forms in court. A case like this is rare however, and I would strongly advise anyone who thinks he or she is in this position to take legal advice just to be certain. Assuming that everything ran smoothly between lawyers, each partner's costs would be likely to be in the region of £500 -£l,000.

• Carol and Michael are an average couple with two children, some savings and some capital in their home and the cost of their divorce depends almost entirely on their ability to agree. If he is open about everything and 'wants to do the right thing', each partner's costs would be unlikely to exceed £5,000. However, the moment he argues over her claim to a share of his company pension or she decides that she wants to 'take him for everything he's got', their costs could multiply two-, three-, four- or five-fold.

• Lucy and Clive who have a large family business, a complicated portfolio of investments and a villa overseas to which they can escape from their £1.5 million home. A divorce case like this really is impossible to estimate: it could be £5,000 a side, it could be £10,000, it could be £30,000. It could easily be more. It all depends on how complex the case becomes and how much the two parties fight. If the case is heard in London, costs can be stratospheric. A top barrister, for example, might charge £25,000, a top accountant even more. The costs of each side could easily reach £200,000.

The only thing that these three couples have in common and should always bear in mind is that the greater the dispute during the divorce, the less there is available for division afterwards. From my own point of view, I try to avoid building up costs. A client who has paid a huge bill out of assets is unlikely to recommend you in the future. Goodwill is important to all of us. Remind your solicitor if you need to do so from time to time. Then remind yourself. There is a price to pay for peace of mind but it might be worth it.

23. Pre-nuptial agreements

Pre-nuptial agreements – a common sense agreement between consenting adults making logical arrangements in case something should go wrong, or the most unromantic start to a loving relationship that is supposed to be for life? Are they just for Hollywood stars and then super-rich or do they have any relevance for the rest of us.

The failure of the marriage of Tom Cruise and Nicole Kidman was the latest in a long line of celebrity relationships where the accountants and lawyers were called in as soon as the marriage guidance counsellors leave the room. Michael Douglas and Catherine Zeta-Jones were reported to have signed a pre-nuptial agreement before their lavish wedding and reception in New York. When Wimbledon legend Boris Becker split acrimoniously with his wife Barbara, Germany's Bild am Sonntag newspaper reported that she had secured a divorce settlement of £10 million, some five times greater than the pre-nuptial agreement they signed when they walked down the aisle in 1993. When Oasis frontman Noel Gallagher decided to end his marriage to party-goer extraordinaire Meg Matthews, he said it was because he fancied a quieter life in his country pile whilst his wife remained enthusiastically committed to having a good time in the hip bars and clubs in London. Even though they signed a pre-nuptial contract agreeing a settlement of £100,000 in the event of a divorce, Meg reportedly wanted her ex to stump up half of his estimated £25 million fortune, made up of cash and houses.

However, it is in the USA where the pre-nuptial agreement is rapidly becoming as important as the engagement ring. The question is whether it has a place in this country and, in particular, for us mere mortals who are not rock superstars or movie-star multi-millionaires. American culture pervades the world; just look at how ubiquitous the McDonald's sign or the Coca-Cola can have become. They're both readily available from Maine to Manchester to Minsk. It doesn't mean, however, that we should welcome all things Stateside with open arms.

Marriage is supposed to be all about showing to the world that you love each other and intend to remain together for the rest of your lives. Even in an age when we have depressingly high divorce statistics, it does seem to me that pre-nuptial agreements are a cold-hearted undermining of this whole concept. It's a bit like having the divorce before the honeymoon. Rather than sealing a loving and lasting relationship with a kiss, a pre-nuptial agreement can deliver the kiss of death to a marriage.

I would go so far as to say that such agreements can actually encourage marital breakdown. How? Well, if part of the agreement includes an installment arrangement of so much cash per year of marriage, as reportedly was the case with Michael Douglas and Catherine Zeta-Jones, then a husband is going to be sorely tempted to throw in the towel at the first sign of fading passion. It will certainly be cheaper!

Pre-nuptial agreements may well have a place in the lives of the Hollywood superstars where both sides might be phenomenally and independently wealthy and want to protect their financial positions in the event of a breakdown. Tinseltown is hardly the best advertisement for the concept of marriage being for life so a pre-marriage contract is probably a practical step to ward-off the gold-diggers.

In my practice I have prepared pre-nuptial agreements to cover specific circumstances:-

• in a second marriage where a wife wants to protect the assets she gained from her first marriage and to ensure her children do not lose out in event of the new relationship foundering.

• when a wealthy woman marries a man with considerably fewer financial resources and wants to protect her assets.

But even in an age when second marriages are so common, such cases are the exception rather than the rule. And there is another important factor to be taken into consideration here. American law is different to that in the United Kingdom. For one thing, a man divorcing his wife in the US knows that he is likely to lose 50% of his estate to his former partner and, therefore, he will want to do all he can to limit his liability. At present, however, pre-nuptial agreements are not legally binding here. Our Courts are not required to follow the terms as set out in a pre-marital agreement. As far as the Court is concerned, it is just another piece of paper to be taken into consideration in deciding a fair and reasonable settlement. In this country, the jurisdiction of the judge is unfettered in reaching a settlement and that, in my opinion, remains by far the best system. The courts have the last word on the division of all matrimonial property and would simply ignore any pre-nuptial agreement it regarded as being in any way unreasonable to either of the parties involved. This is particularly so in regards to maintenance and the housing of any children of the marriage. For example, a court may order the transfer of property from one spouse to the other, regardless of whose name it is legally in.

The situation is very different in the case of couples who chose to live together without the formality of marriage. Co-habitation agreements are legally binding contracts and are enforceable as long as the couple remain unmarried. The popular belief that long-standing but unmarried couples have rights as common law husband and wife is a myth!

So pre-nuptial agreements may have their place in the heady world of the super-rich and the relationship fickle environment of showbusiness, but do they have any relevance for the rest of us?

Interestingly, there are moves afoot which may see them being given legal standing in the UK. A Government Green Paper on ' Supporting Families' contains a proposal that pre-nuptial agreements and contracts be given legal status. The proposal is that they should be binding on those who wish to use them. Importantly, however, they would not be binding if the couple go on to have a child or children. In those circumstances, the court would be able to take charge of the financial resources unfettered by any prior agreement

PART V
What About the Children

24. Children – be reasonable

Changes to the law have done away with the outdated concepts of custody and access and removed one of the most contentious, acrimonious elements of marital breakdown – what happens to the children! And with 142,457 children aged under 16 in families where the parents divorced in 2000, the scale of the problem is evident.

The arrival of the Children Act brought many welcome changes. Divorce cases involving children no longer have mandatory orders and the usual principle to be adopted is that no order will be made in respect of the children unless it is necessary. Custody has been abolished. Both parents retain parental responsibility for their children. Access has been abolished. Instead, the children will have contact with their parents. They will reside with one parent or may reside with both on a split basis if that is appropriate. Their wishes will be taken into account. Since the Children Act has come into force one big area of argument has been removed: who will retain custody and who will give it up. In my view it is a master stroke: the relief that people express when they realise that they do not have to worry about custody is quite tangible. On the whole they can usually agree periods when the children are to see both of them and on the whole they can reach agreement about where the children are to be based. Of course, from time to time one comes across the intransigent person who is incapable of objectivity when considering what is best for the child; in such cases the courts are there to assist. So, to a great extent, the Children Act has achieved its aim of removing the pain, worry and bitterness over children's future - but not wholly. I think it would be unwise to consider that any law could do this because people are human beings and not emotionless robots. The children are always going to be an area of contention. Both of you must be reasonable, prepared to compromise and to think what is best for the child, not what is best for you.

You may not like your partner but a child's view of his or her parent is totally different. He or she will have love and trust for that parent which is capable of transcending even the most dreadful scenes which he or she may have witnessed. And a child prevented from seeing a parent they still love will eventually turn that resentment against the one trying to enforce the unenforceable. So, in the end reasonableness pays!

In my opinion the welfare of children is absolutely the most important area of divorce law. The courts are there if reasonable agreement between partners cannot be reached. There are lawyers who can become involved and the Court Welfare Services, however strained the system, are also available. It is important to remember that with regard to children no order is ever permanent. If circumstances alter, the court can reconsider the position of children in the light of the new arrangements. The court is always the final arbiter. With this in mind, there should be no reason why parties cannot reach a reasonable and sensible compromise, agreeing arrangements which are in the best possible interests for their children. The following chapters concern the role of children during their parents' divorce.

25. Step families

Within the first decade of the 21st Century, the traditional family in Britain will be a thing of the past, an idiosyncrasy to be written about and pored over by future historians and social researchers. Well, that's what some people are forecasting. According to some powerful and perhaps disturbing research by the family help charity, 'Parentline', by 2010 the majority of children will be being brought up in step-families or by single parents. The organisation says that the situation is an 'inevitable' result of the rising number of divorce cases and fewer people getting married. It is the children of those broken relationships, their upbringing and future well being that is the paramount concern of the law but it will need maturity and selflessness on the behalf of parents to ensure this happens with the least rancour and bitterness. Researchers for 'Parentline' say that a change in social attitudes means that more parents in marriages which are on the rocks, are no longer staying together 'for the sake of the children.'

The prediction that the traditional family will soon be a minority in British society is based on research in north London carried out by the Office of National Statistics and the Policy Studies Institute. Some campaigners for the traditional family blame Government policy for failing to support marriage. They claim, for instance, that sex education in schools no longer mentions marriage and that the Government does not admit there is any difference between a married family unit and any other. There are also other acknowledged pressures; financial, career stress, the juggling of work demands and home life, the changing relationship between men and women in general, more liberal social attitudes etc.

'Parentline' published the research in a document, called 'Young People and Family Change.' It also says that children are often those who suffer the most when the marriage of their parents is dissolved. Among the complaints voiced by children is of having to live with their mother's new partner who they actively dislike, of being used to 'spy' during visits to the separated parent. I believe that in this country we have developed an enlightened and entirely proper approach to the issue of child welfare in marriage breakdown. The introduction of the Children Act in 1991 did away with the whole outdated question of 'ownership' of a child, removed the concept of custody and ruled that it was the interests of the child, not the parents, which were to guide the court's decisions.

This is an example of where our law is far preferable to that in the United States. There the rights of parents are still paramount, sometimes to the obvious detriment of the child concerned. I can still vividly remember television pictures of a child being literally torn from the arms of its adopted mother of many years standing to be handed back by court officers to the natural mother it barely knew.

In this country, courts have to refer to a Welfare Check-List when making decisions about where and with whom a child should live in the event of the breakdown in the parent's relationship. These include:-

• the wishes and feelings of the child
• the child's physical, emotional and educational needs
• the likely effect of any change in his or her circumstances
• the child's age, sex, background and relevant characteristics
• any harm the child has suffered or is at risk of suffering
• how capable each parent is of meeting the needs of the child

In the majority of cases I deal with, parents do reach an agreement which is in the best interests of their child, even though it may go against their own personal desires. In some cases however, where the wife is termed 'implacably hostile' as a result of the position she finds herself in, the resulting traumas can be truly distressing.

American academics have now identified a condition known as Parental Alienation Syndrome, where the resident parent in a dispute persistently brainwashes the child against the other parent to the extent that his or her previous loving relationship is ended. In the UK a new, single - issue political party was launched to campaign for the equal treatment of divorcing couples in relation to shared parenting of their children. The Equal Parenting Party claimed to be drawing support throughout the country. Clearly, this demonstrates that no matter how forward thinking our legislation, there will always be parents who feel they are being denied their rights in relation to their children.

If the prediction that the step-family will be the norm in 10 years time turns out to be true, then the pressures will not just be on the courts but also on parents who must be unselfish enough to make decisions in the real best interests of their children, not of themselves.

26. Suffer the children

The sheer number of children affected by divorce represents a disturbing legacy for society, not least because of their future ability of those children to form stable, long-term relationships. These children will have seen their parents fight, scream and cry. They will feel upset, uncertain as to what the future holds, and often they will feel torn in their loyalty to both parents. Even if Mum and Dad save the crockery throwing and accusations of intolerable behaviour for those times when the kids are out of the house, even the youngest or least perceptive child is soon going to realise that all is not well. So just what can a divorcing couple do to minimise the pain felt by their children?

Rule number one clearly is not to involve the children in the row. There is a real possibility that they will already feel that it is somehow their fault, and being dragged into the middle of it all will only intensify this feeling of guilt. What children need is constant reassurance that they are not to blame, that they are still loved by both parents and, whatever may happen in the future, that this will always be the case. What they don't need is pressure from either parent to take sides. To subject young children to this would be bordering on abuse, and in practice would probably only serve to swing their loyalty the other way.

So a united front must be presented in all discussions and decisions that involve the children. If a child discovers that his parents are arguing over his future it will be upsetting to say the least, and if he has an opinion to express he may feel unable to do so through fear of alienating one or other parent. Remember too that divorce is just as bewildering for the children as for you. So be honest with them, short of burdening them with all the less salubrious details. Don't for instance tell the children that Daddy has been misbehaving. Just tell them that Mummy and Daddy are no longer happy living together.

Children are almost always tempted to try to push their parents back together. This rarely works out, and it's easier for them to come to terms with the divorce if they have some idea of the reason why. However much you might like a clean break, only in the most exceptional circumstances would a court sever all links between one parent and his or her children, so the more civilised the divorce, the better for everyone in the long run.

So what of the arrangements for the children, that minefield of an area where emotions can and often do reach boiling point? How do you decide who should live where? How are such arrangements agreed? How much, if at all, should children be consulted? Again the secret of avoiding unnecessary conflict is compromise. It will not be easy, but you must try to sit down and talk everything through as rationally as possible. You've got to be brave and tackle the problems head on. Having hysterics, flying off the handle and tantrums in the home just will not help. If you stay calm and cool and don't get involved in arguments it will be better ultimately for everyone. Try to get it sorted out as quickly as possible. Where discussion drags on there is always more anger and more hurt.

Consider who will be best able to meet the children's emotional, financial and educational needs. Consider who will be able to provide them with the stability that is so important in the early years. And consider the practicalities of all possible arrangements. However insistent your husband may be that he wants the children with him, if he works shifts or his job involves a great deal of travelling, it is extremely unlikely that any court would decide that the children should reside with him. Remember, any agreement you might make between you will have to be approved by the courts in the end. The main point here is that however much it may help you personally, your only consideration must be how the best interests of the children will be served. Never, ever, use the children as bargaining tools. Children are capable of understanding more than you think and it is easy for parents to use them as pawns in negotiation without realising just how painful this is. And if the final decision over the children does end up in court, this will certainly go against you.

For example, the man who threatens to demand a residence order in his favour unless he has unreasonably regular contact or she accepts a low rate of maintenance could well end up much worse off than if they had reached a satisfactory compromise. Almost certainly the children will end up with her, he will be made to pay a satisfactory level of maintenance and his threatening demands could mean that he is given only very limited contact.

The secret is to be reasonable. Try at all costs to sort it out before it reaches a court where the final decision might not suit either of you or the children. While divorce is rarely going to be a pleasant business, with determination from both sides that the children will not suffer, it is possible for them to come through it all with their self-confidence and love for you both still intact. However tough it gets, that must be the ultimate goal of every parent.

28. Dad's the word....

Sir Bob Geldof has never been one to keep his own counsel on issues about which he feels passionately. The driving force behind the Live Aid concerts, campaigner against Third World debt, he has turned his attention to a more intensely personal topic but one, once again, where he is echoing the concerns of a wider audience.

Sir Bob, whose court battles with his ex-wife, the late Paula Yates over residence of their three daughters, were bitter and acrimonious, has launched a passionate defence of lone fathers. He claims that courts in the UK are wrong to favour mothers over fathers when it comes to deciding where children should live when a marriage breaks-down.

He has urged the British legal system to acknowledge that men can often make the better carers when parents divorce.

" When one partner leaves the other, the children should remain with the partner who has not left. To suggest that the interests of the children are nearly always best served by the presence of the mother is just not empirically true."

" Men adore and love their children as much as women, though they may display it in different ways. Courts and judges need to understand that not all men are brutal indifferent bores and women ministering angels," he said in a magazine interview.

The case of Sir Bob and his ex-wife may have commanded the headlines but his appeal is undoubtedly one that finds resonance with many fathers.

Just consider the facts. In 2000 there were 141,135 divorces and these involved 142,457 children aged under 16. The position in which Sir Bob found himself on the break-up of his marriage is one shared by countless thousands of men; men who don't stop loving their children even though they have fallen out of love with their children's mother.

These men don't suddenly stop being good fathers.

So is Sir Bob right? Do father's get a raw deal?

At one time, it was almost automatic that, in the event of divorce, the children went to live with their mother. It was just assumed, by judges, social workers and probably society at large, that that was the 'natural' way of things.

Children, particularly young ones, had special and deep psychological bonds with their mothers that it was thought wrong and harmful to break; fathers were seen as breadwinners and not natural home-makers.

There is little doubt that this led to much pain and heartache among those fathers who often felt they had done nothing to lead to the failure of the marriage but were then being doubly punished by losing daily contact with their children.

A historic ruling in the Appeal Court in 1991 by Dame Justice Butler-Sloss backed a father's claim that his daughter should live with him and ordered a lower court to reconsider their earlier judgement in favour of the mother.

This case set a precedent, denying women the near-automatic right to have children live with them when a relationship broke down. Above all, this case led to a re-examination of how the courts dealt with contested residency. The priority was to come to a decision that was in the best interests of the children involved. Nothing more and nothing less.

It is estimated that anything from 30% to 50% of all fathers lose touch with their children within a couple of years of a divorce. It is a shocking statistic that must cause disbelief among the many millions of men who live for their children.

Many men still feel as though they are treated as second class citizens when it comes to residence of the children or contact arrangements with them.

However, experience shows that if a man puts together a cogent and reasoned argument about why he should have residency of his children, then the courts are prepared to look at it in an even-handed way.

Successive governments tell us that 'fatherhood is for life.' But if a man is expected, rightly, to provide financially for his children then is it not only fair and equitable that the ' fatherhood for life' principle be considered when the question of where the children will live comes to be made?

There is little doubt that the position for fathers today is much better than a decade ago. Much of that is down to the changes that have taken place in society and how the roles and rights of men and women have developed.

For instance, it is not uncommon today for the wife to be the breadwinner whilst the man stays at home as house-husband to take daily care of the children. If such a relationship ends, then who should the children live with?

The essential principle is that children are not 'owned' by anyone. They are individuals with their own rights and needs. More than ever, courts listen to the opinions of children caught up in relationship breakdowns.

If a teenage child, for instance, is determinedly opposed to contact with one or other parents, then a court is highly unlikely to make an order that has very little chance of being obeyed. With younger children, their wishes are still taken into account, depending on their age, but they are not decisive in themselves.

Of course, the best solution to this question is an amicable agreement by both parties as to what is in the best interest of the child. After all, just because two people decide they can no longer live together doesn't turn them into unfit parents overnight!

However, when agreement proves impossible, the courts are now more prepared than ever to consider the father's case in a sympathetic manner.

Things may not yet be perfect - in such difficult circumstances as divorce the 'perfect' solution is not always possible – but I believe the law has now achieved a much fairer balance.

It may not be ' a man's world' in such cases but 'dad' is no longer a dirty word when it comes to decide where a child of divorce should live.

28. Children - rights of contact

To some extent a divorce lawyer's work is seasonal. In the weeks before Christmas there is a noticeable drop in the number of new instructions. People are affected by the approach of Christmas and are too busy buying presents and preparing for Christmas Day to consider the state of the marriage. Immediately following the Christmas period there is a significant increase in injunctions arising out of violence and, following an enforced stay together, many couples decide to make the break.

The approach of the school holidays and in particular the onset of the long summer holidays gives rise to numerous problems such as when, where and for how long does each parent spend with the children. Divorce lawyers are beset by anxious parents raising queries. Can I take my children abroad? If so for how long? Do I need my partner's consent? If he/she refuses then what? The obvious and most sensible solution in cases like this, to avoid breaking the law, is to sit down and talk. This is easier said than done of course, but it is by far the cheapest and quickest way of reaching agreement. Unfortunately, as I find over and over again, being sensible, talking and reaching a compromise does not often happen until the courts intervene. Quite why this is so I have not been able to understand. I am frequently approached by people who are prepared to spend a lot of money arguing whether or not their children can go on that two-week holiday to Spain.

If the matter cannot be resolved between the parties or by solicitors in negotiation then frequently there is an emergency application to the court and the judge decides what to do. Usually the holiday to Spain will take place and a lot of money has been spent arguing about the apparently inevitable. Whether the children will enjoy their Spanish holiday is very often the last consideration of the warring parents but it will be the first consideration of the judge.

Will they be adequately looked after; are the arrangements sensible; if an emergency arises, will the children be safe? If the answers are all yes then of course the holiday will take place. In fact, under the provisions of the Children Act a parent with a residence order can take a child abroad for twenty-eight days without needing the other parent's consent.

The more divorce work that I do, the more I realise there are no winners or losers. It is all about being reasonable and reaching a sensible agreement. The emotions which can cloud and seriously affect your judgement are non-productive, affect only yourself and do not make for a long-term relationship which at the end of the day is preferred to one of constant war. Of course marriages collapse because the relationship has broken down. Love and affection are no longer there. However, that is no excuse for reason and common sense not being applied by both parties where children are involved.

PART VI

And Don't Forget
the Rest

29. Grandparents - the forgotten casualties of divorce

The main concern of anyone whose work is connected with divorce, whether he or she is a solicitor, a counsellor or a social worker, is that the welfare of the children should be paramount. Around 140,000 children suffer the feelings of confusion and loss as a result of divorce each year, and it is right that priority is given to helping them. The system then takes care of the dividing couples themselves. The legal process ensures that both partners are generally as well provided for as they can be from whatever joint assets they possess, and agencies such as Relate are there to give emotional support and guidance. The system is by no means perfect, but in the main the channels exist whereby help can be provided for those who are directly involved.

More often than not, though, a divorce will have a tremendously disturbing effect on a number of other people too. And no-one more so than the grandparents. Not only do they have to watch as their son's or daughter's life is torn apart but, in the case of the paternal grandparents, they also have to face up to the very real possibility of never seeing their grandchildren again. Unless a strong bond has been built up between a mother and her former parents-in-law, it is fairly common for paternal grandparents to be forced to lose touch as and when the father does. In some cases where a father does make use of his contact rights, visitors are only grudgingly allowed as a kind of trade for maintenance payments. Deep down, the former wife would prefer to make a clean break from her past life, so to keep in regular contact with her former husband's parents as well only serves to make things all that more difficult.

• The problems experienced by Adam and Marie, a couple in their late fifties, are by no means unusual. When their son Ben was divorced from his wife Sophie three years ago, they did their utmost to keep in touch, offering to come round and babysit whenever she needed a break from looking after two demanding children on her own. Eventually, though, Sophie decided that this arrangement was preventing her from starting a new life apart from Ben so she moved back to her hometown, 150 miles away. Ben was allowed to visit the children and Sophie would occasionally bring them down to see his parents, but her trips were infrequent. A year later, having not seen their grandchildren for a while, Marie rang her former daughter-in-law and suggested that they should visit her this time. Sophie told her that she was engaged to be married to someone new, and that as Ben had not been to visit for six months, it might be better if she could break off all the ties she had with her old life. Adam and Marie were devastated, but realised that to try to visit against Sophie's wishes might well create friction, thereby upsetting their grandchildren. Not wishing to be the cause of any further distress in the two children's young lives, they resigned themselves to sending cards at Christmas and birthdays.

Thousands of grandparents go through similarly awful experiences every year and, in truth, there can never be an ideal solution to the problem. On the one hand, one can sympathise with Sophie's feelings. She genuinely felt the need to break away if she was ever going to start afresh, and visits from her former husband's parents could well have been embarrassing for both them and her new husband. On the other hand though, these children were 'flesh and blood' relatives of Adam and Marie, who doted on the grand-children in the way that all grandparents do. The children's deep affection for Grandma and Grandad was clear.

This is a particularly sad case because even though everyone concerned acted in a civilised manner the problem could not be resolved. Perhaps if Adam and Marie had been less sensitive to Sophie's wishes (or more determined to keep in touch - it depends how you look at it) there might still be some contact today. There are other cases of course, where the lack of contact is down to sheer bloody-mindedness on the part of the residential parent. Having been hurt by the divorce, he or she takes revenge by obstructing the grandparents' access at every possible opportunity, often to the detriment of the children's happiness.

Is there any legal action that a grandparent - or indeed any other close relative can take in a situation like this? In the past, contact orders were occasionally granted to grandparents, but only rarely.

Since the implementation of the Children Act, grandparents are amongst those who are able, with leave of the court, to apply for a contact order. The court then makes its own decision, having referred to the checklist that among other things requires the child's own wishes and emotional needs to be taken into consideration. The key to its decision is whether or not the children will benefit from the order that is made. Even the child him- or herself, if considered mature enough, can apply to the court for leave to make an application for a contact order.

30. Living Together

Not that many years ago, sharing a house as an unmarried couple was considered to be an act of rebellion, a rejection of the convention of society. Recently, however, I read of one celebrity who had decided to get married because that had now become the more unconventional thing to do! There was also the case of a grandfather, with distinctly old-fashioned values, who offered each of his four grand-daughters £1,000 each on their wedding day only if they had not lived with a man before marriage.

If one leaves aside the moral issue, which clearly many people are quite willing to do, living together can be a valuable trial run before marriage. Faults and irritating habits that can be concealed during the occasional night out are impossible to disguise when sharing bedrooms and bathrooms. So for some 'living together for a while' has become as acceptable as an engagement. And that's fine, just as long as the relationship either dies a relatively quick death or develops into something more permanent. It's when a couple have been living together for a significant length of time and then decide to call it a day that problems can arise.

The old saying that a little knowledge can be a dangerous thing was never more true than it is where cohabitation is concerned. Every pub in the land has a bar room lawyer who will confidently tell you that you're entitled to a quarter/half/all of his or her worldly goods if you've lived together for six/twelve/twenty-four months - take any combination you like, they're all wrong! Although there are moves to have such relationships given legal status, the fact of the matter is that the law doesn't yet recognise 'common law marriages', something that becomes only too clear when the woman is referred to in court as 'the mistress', as often happens. In short, there are no statutory laws relating to cohabitation, not even a formula for agreeing the division of assets.

The law relating to cohabitees is entirely different from the law relating to married couples as far as property rights are concerned , although issues involving children are dealt with in a similar way. It is important to remember that cohabitees mean any couple who live together and that includes those of the same sex.

Couples who live together do separate, though, and the courts do have to decide how any disputed assets should be divided. Technically in law, any property continues to belong to the person who owned it before the relationship began, the person who actually paid for it. So if a man owns a house and moves his girlfriend in and she makes no contribution and the relationship subsequently breaks down, there is no question but that the house remains his property and the girlfriend has no claim on it, whether there are children or not. The main consideration therefore -and I use the example of the man's house only because this is the most common scenario - is what contribution the woman made to their assets. This can be financial or physical, but it must be proven. This is an area of the law where there is massive injustice. Very often lawyers will enter into convoluted arguments so their clients can walk out of the relationship with something. Maintenance for themselves however is out of the question, although child support must be paid. Sometimes, a property 'loaned' by the man until a child reaches 18 is the only outcome for a woman who may have spent years with him.

Perhaps we would be better if we were to adopt a system like those used in the United States or Australia, where a relationship that is generally recognised as being that of husband and wife is rated in much the same way as a 'legitimate' marriage. As mentioned earlier, there are moves underway in Parliament to introduce new legislation that would provide legal status for such relationships. However, until it does become law, the only advice I can offer to anyone in a medium to long-term cohabiting relationship is to be aware of how significantly reduced your rights are and, if at all possible, get your name on the title deeds or get married.

Plan with your partner what you would do in the event of a split and enter into a cohabitation agreement. Normalise as much as you can of your financial arrangements. Save your income, have joint building society and bank accounts, insurance policies and property. Both of you should make wills. Do not live like an ostrich - you are at significant risk.. Think how things should be sorted out if you break up. If he won't be reasonable now, chances are he'll be a heck of a lot worse then.

31. Where there's a will, there's a way

When it comes to death and divorce, we as a nation score pretty badly on the international scale of things. Our divorce rate is the highest in Europe, and British men are more likely than most to die prematurely from the primary western world killers such as coronaries and strokes. Since divorce is recognised as being one of the most stressful events in a person's life, these two facts may not be entirely unrelated. But that is not why I mention them together here.

I do so to highlight a problem that could well be on the increase, a problem that causes all sorts of difficulties for thousands of women and children in the UK, and, worst of all, a problem that really shouldn't exist at all. That problem is men who either fail to make a will, or assume that the one they made years ago is still valid, when it almost certainly isn't. The man who dies intestate (without having a will) when he has a wife and children shows a tremendous lack of consideration for his dependents. Worse still is the man who not only fails to make a will in the first place but then divorces, remarries or cohabits and dies. The former leaves his wife and children who will eventually receive his estate, possibly tied up in trusts he could never have imagined or wanted. The latter leaves a wife, ex-wife, or cohabitee, quite possibly two sets of children, and one awful mess.

The arguments over who is entitled to what share of his estate could rage on for years. What rights do the children from his first marriage have? Are these rights affected if the mother has remarried? What about the children of his second marriage, the eldest of whom was the product of his new wife's first marriage? The legal costs involved in sorting it all out could theoretically outweigh the value of his entire estate! A will is therefore essential, but even this is not a straightforward matter. Marrying or remarrying automatically revokes a previous will and, on divorce, a bequest to a previous spouse becomes void. A cohabitee of course does not automatically inherit, although if she is a dependant she can apply to the court for her fair share. Let's look at a fairly typical example.

Andrew is in his mid-thirties, he is onto his second marriage and has to make fairly substantial payments every week towards the maintenance of his first wife and their two children. He made a will when he first married, but either through a lack of understanding of his legal position or simple negligence, he hasn't bothered to update it yet. Upon his sudden death, this glaring omission in his financial arrangements turns the whole situation into a nightmare for those he leaves behind. The payments that his first wife relied upon for the mortgage dry up straightaway. His second wife also encounters immediate financial difficulties as there are no longer two salaries coming into the household. The will that he so carefully made out ten years ago in favour of his first wife is now invalid, so everyone has to wait, debts mounting up, until the situation can be resolved.

What could he have done instead? While it's impossible to be too specific, he clearly should have made better provision for both of his families. Most of his assets would almost certainly be left to his new wife, but certain arrangements could and should have been made to secure the future of his first family. A life insurance policy, covering maintenance payments in the event of his death, wouldn't have been a bad idea for a start! Responsibilities like children from a previous marriage cannot be ignored. Even if he had left everything to his second wife, his first wife could still make a claim from the estate, assuming she is a dependent and on behalf of the children. It's a complex business, so proper legal advice is essential.

To ask a couple who are in the process of a painful divorce to discuss the content and validity of a will might seem a little like pouring petrol over a smouldering fire. And if one partner is still angry over the cause of the break-up - their spouse's adultery for instance - it is unlikely that any provision made in a revised will is going to be particularly generous. But if there are children involved or maintenance payments to be made careful planning and a new will are essential. For if one or the other partner should die shortly after the divorce, the pain that will be caused to those left behind by lack of a will, or a valid will, could be almost as bad as the divorce or the death itself.

32. Violence within the home - the legal remedies

Divorce lawyers have stories of extreme violence told to them practically every day of the week by women seeking help through the form of a non-molestation order and/or occupation orders on the house. We hear of the number of violent men from all socio-economic groups who think nothing of slapping their partners if there are no convenient pieces of furniture to break instead. It is relatively common to meet bruised and battered women with bitten faces or broken jaws, all seeking urgent help from their lawyers. At its worst, violence in the home involves wives paying the ultimate price. In England and Wales, for example, of 224 female homicide victims, 47% were killed by current or former partners. This compares with just 8% of the 426 male homicides that year being killed by their partners.

The legal process is designed to assist quickly and in fact it does help within limits. Divorce lawyers are trained to work speedily and out of normal office hours. The court system is geared up to get a person seeking an order in front of a court as quickly as possible; the whole process can be carried out and an order obtained usually at the least for " non molestation", the Court usually being reluctant to have a recalcitrant spouse removed from the home without the opportunity of giving him his say, and him being served within a day.

• Susan and Tom had been married for ten years and had two children aged eight and five. Throughout the entire marriage Tom, who liked to drink, had felt able to hit out at his wife, usually when he came home from the pub, but not always. During the marriage she had sustained a black eye, a broken finger, a torn lip and bruises on her body. She felt however that for much of the marriage he had been quite normal but then 'something would come over him' - he would change and become very angry and let rip. The children had witnessed the violence. It was easy to cope with most of the time but on a couple of occasions she had to spend time in bed to recover. This time, however, he had gone too far. He had literally broken both her nose and jaw and she felt she could not carry on. She sought legal advice after discharging herself from hospital. She obtained her order and began divorce proceedings. Within two weeks Tom, now suitably ashamed and embarrassed and facing the break-up of his marriage and the loss of his home, vowed never to beat her again. He sent her flowers and he cried in front of her, showing his remorse. Apologetically, she instructed her lawyers that she had decided to withdraw proceedings 'for the sake of the children'.

Susan took the easy option which was to stay put. The children are always a consideration but there are other factors such as security, financial stability and the emotional commitment to a permanent relationship which, on the whole, has its good days. Susan made her decision having had time to think and in the throws of recovery from physical pain and substantial emotional blackmail - 'if you don't come back I'll kill myself' - she was too weak and worn out to continue.

Those who seek a divorce usually do so when they have considered every possible alternative and have reached a reasoned, albeit painful, conclusion that life cannot go on as it is. Unfortunately those who seek emergency orders do so out of immediate panic and fear, by their very nature are obtained at a time of greatest need. Even then it is by no means perfect; to many it is merely a piece of paper and a major criticism of the system is that there is little or no obvious backup from the police. The stock phrase is usually 'go and get an order, love, there's nothing we can do without it'

A desperate women will not know whether this is true or false - in fact it is false.

If you are abused and battered the law is there to help you and to keep you as safe as possible. The police should be contacted immediately and at the very least they will ensure that there is no breach of the peace. In serious cases they will institute criminal proceedings. Civil orders can stop your partner assaulting or molesting you and can keep him away from your home (and out of his home, whether he owns it outright or jointly, and whether you are married or not). If he breaches the injunction he can be sent to prison for contempt. In certain cases the police can be ordered to arrest him immediately and bring him before the court.

These remedies do work but only with a positive commitment to them and a determination to see it through. The easy way out may seem at the time to capitulate and start again - that is, until the next time. My advice to those who are suffering is to think positive and do something about it before there is a next time. The next time may be the last time!